NUTS AND BERRIES OF CALIFORNIA

NUTS AND BERRIES OF CALIFORNIA

Tips and Recipes for Gatherers

Christopher Nyerges

FALCONGUIDES

GUILFORD, CONNECTICUT
HELENA, MONTANA

For Paul Campbell, who died in September 2014.

FALCONGUIDES®

An imprint of Rowman & Littlefield

Falcon, FalconGuides, and Outfit Your Mind are registered trademarks of Rowman & Littlefield

Distributed by National Book Network

Copyright © 2015 by Rowman & Littlefield

All photos by Christopher Nyerges unless otherwise noted.

British Library Cataloguing-in-Publication Information Is Available

Library of Congress Cataloging-in-Publication Data

Nyerges, Christopher, author.
  Nuts and berries of California : tips and recipes for gatherers / Christopher Nyerges.
    pages cm
  Includes index.
  ISBN 978-1-4930-0184-2
  1. Nuts—California. 2. Berries—California. 3. Wild plants, Edible—California. I. Title.
  SB355.5.C2N94 2015
  634'.509794—dc23

                                    2015001973

ISBN 978-1-4930-1491-0 (e-book)

∞™ The paper used in this publication meets the minimum requirements of American National Standard for Information Sciences—Permanence of Paper for Printed Library Materials, ANSI/NISO Z39.48-1992.

CONTENTS

Horticulturally Introduced Plants

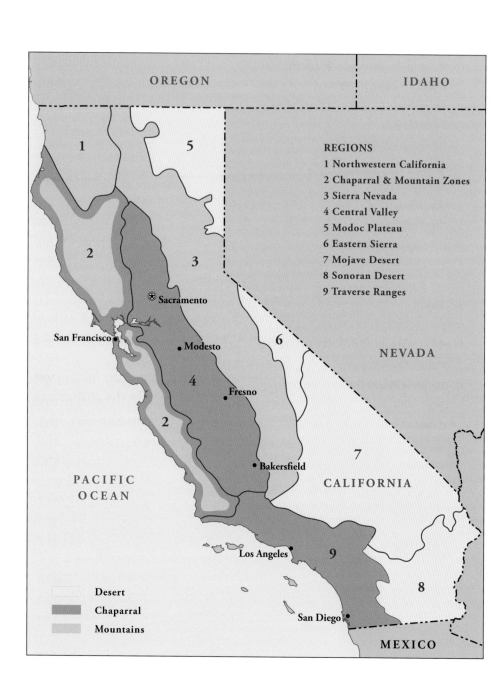

OREGON   IDAHO

1   5

                              REGIONS
                              1 Northwestern California
                              2 Chaparral & Mountain Zones
                              3 Sierra Nevada
2   3   4 Central Valley
                              5 Modoc Plateau
                              6 Eastern Sierra
                              7 Mojave Desert
                              8 Sonoran Desert
      ⊛ Sacramento   9 Traverse Ranges

San Francisco •
                              6
                                          NEVADA
          • Modesto

              4
                   • Fresno

        2
                                      CALIFORNIA
              • Bakersfield

PACIFIC
OCEAN

                              9
      Los Angeles •   7

                                          8

          • San Diego

          Desert
          Chaparral   MEXICO
          Mountains

FOREWORD

When I was a child in Oregon, I learned to follow the local Native Americans and eat what they ate. I learned how to pick and eat huckleberries, still my favorite fruit. Even now, every fall I store my huckleberries so I can make it through the winter. I cannot imagine getting through a winter without huckleberries.

I have learned about many other edible plants as well. When I came to California, many years ago, I encountered people who told me the berries I picked were poisonous. I have been told not to pick berries by forest rangers, who claimed the law forbids it. I was fortunate to be trained by the Chumash people for more than fourteen years in medicinal and edible uses of plants. I have had many great interactions with California Indians and eaten many wild foods with them.

California desperately needs Christopher Nyerges's book on edible fruits and nuts. This book can help us overcome our fear and lack of knowledge about edible wild foods. Christopher has a gentle and kind way of teaching that should appeal to everyone.

It is important for us to eat what grows locally, since the local plants help us adapt to the changing seasons and conditions. In the spring, I eat gooseberries. In the summer, I eat holly leaf cherries and elderberries. In the fall, I eat acorns and huckleberries. I gather enough acorns and huckleberries for the winter as well. In the winter, I eat toyon berries and my gathered acorns and huckleberries.

California has many unique plants that provide great food for us to eat. I especially enjoy screwbean mesquite. The cherry-date flavor of California palm fruit is also appealing. I encourage everyone to increase the variety of their diets by eating a variety of fruits, vegetables, and nuts. Variety increases health by giving us a variety of phytonutrients. I grow toyon berries in my yard and eat them. I eat every edible berry, nut, and fruit that I find when I am hiking or running in the wild.

This book will help you learn how to eat what is in the wild, and increase your health by increasing the variety of your diet.

—Dr. James David Adams, Jr.,
University of Southern California,
School of Pharmacy, Los Angeles;
Coauthor of *Healing with Medicinal Plants of the West*
(with Cecilia Garcia)

ACKNOWLEDGMENTS

As usual, a book is not the product of one person. Lots of bright folks helped me with this project. Paul Campbell made lots of useful suggestions during the inception of this book, and offered lots of tips and hints for what to include. Dr. James Adams read the text, offered suggestions, and wrote the foreword. Dr. James Bauml read the HIPs section for accuracy and made good suggestions. Mickey Long assisted me with the environmental section. And this project couldn't have been completed without the assistance of the photographers who participated. These include Zoya Akulova, Aaron Arthur, Daniel Baird, Pascal Baudar, Debra Cook, John Doyen, Trent Draper, Julie Kierstead Nelson, Jean Pawek, Vernon Smith, Helen Sweaney, and especially Rick Adams.

INTRODUCTION

FORAGING CALIFORNIA'S NUTS AND BERRIES

This book is all about the wild nuts and berries of California. Both nuts and berries are the seed-bearing fruiting bodies of a plant. Both nuts and berries are fruits, but there is a difference. Berries are typically very fleshy, with one or more seeds—large or small—inside the fruit. The nuts are not fleshy fruits, but dry fruits, often with a hard shell, and include walnuts, pecans, hickory nuts, and acorns. In other words, this book is all about fruits—two specific types of fruits of California plants.

Most people already know blackberries. The blackberry is perhaps the most universally known berry in the entire world. When families say they're going out to collect berries, chances are they mean blackberries. And just about everyone knows what a walnut is—even the wild black walnut with its thick shell.

These are just two of the fruits found in this book, as well as others that are equally as common, though not as widely known.

HOW TO USE THIS GUIDE

This book is divided into two main sections:

1. **Native** nuts and berries
2. **Introduced** nuts and berries

The **Native** section includes those nuts and berries that are most common, and which you are most likely to encounter. We've chosen to not mention any plants if they are now rare, even if they were once used for food by indigenous people. We've also chosen to not mention any berries or nuts that are very localized, or those that are very marginal foods and were really only eaten when there wasn't much else available. All plants are organized alphabetically by common name.

The **Introduced** section (Horticulturally Introduced Plants, or HIPs) includes a few plants that are widely distributed and planted in the urban areas, and that survive so well when they go feral that they seem to be natives.

We've also included some fleshy fruits, like the prickly pear, which are not normally called "berries."

The point of this book is to direct people into the field so they can begin enjoying *common* nuts and fruits, and incorporate them into their diets—today! The nuts and fruits included are not rare, are fairly widespread, and are relative easy to identify.

Not all berries and nuts are edible. Though deadly poisonous berries and nuts are certainly not common, you should never eat any wild food or wild plant until you've identified it as an edible species. Just eat what you know.

We hope this helps your enjoyment of the outdoors, and we'd love to hear from you, whether it's your questions, comments, or suggestions.

Note: spp. (plural species) is the simpler way to refer to many or all the species of a genus, and is used throughout this guide.

WHY GATHER NUTS AND BERRIES?

People take to the woods and backyards in search of wild nuts and berries for many reasons. Most folks get hooked on the idea that you can just go outside, commune with nature in the way that's best for you, and then find a snack or lunch. Food is everywhere. I recall, when I began learning how to forage around age 12 that it seemed terribly exciting to know how to find food that was always there, and that Native Americans had known about and used for millennia. It was like peeling back a mysterious fog and penetrating into the deep past for a skill that would be with me forever in this modern world.

Of course, the collection and use of wild edibles has gained popularity in the last few decades because more people are aware of the fragility of our modern methods of agriculture, not to mention all the support systems that get food from the farm to your local store. It makes practical sense to learn about local wild plants, and it also makes sense to grow at least a little of your own food.

Many folks realize that food from the wild is often nutritionally better than what they have been purchasing from their supermarkets. Nutritional data from the US Department of Agriculture (USDA) supports this idea. Wild foods really are nutritionally superior to the most common cultivated fruits and vegetables that you find in every supermarket.

In his book *Participating in Nature*, Thomas Elpel has created a unique chart to give a perspective on the sheer number of edible, medicinal, and poisonous plants. First, almost every plant with known ethnobotanical uses can be used medicinally. Even some otherwise toxic plants can be used medicinally if you know the right doses and proper application. So yes, medicine is everywhere. But nearly two-thirds of these plants are neither poisonous nor used for food for various reasons.

About 10–15 percent of wild foods consist of berries or fruits, and timing is everything. Unlike greens, which you can usually find year-round, fruits and berries are typically available only seasonally, so if you want some during other parts of the year, you'll need to dry them or make jams or preserves. This includes blackberries, elderberries, toyon, and all other berries described in this book. These provide sugars and flavor, and like greens, you would not make a meal entirely from fruits and berries.

Another small category of wild foods consists of seeds and nuts. This includes grass seeds, pine nuts, mesquite, screwbeans, carob, acorns, and many others. It is in this small category, maybe 5 percent of wild foods, where you obtain the carbohydrates, oils, and sometimes proteins that constitute the "staff of life." Though these are not available all year, some have a longer harvest time than others. Others may have a harvest period as short as two weeks. Many grass seeds simply fall to the ground and are eaten by animals. Fortunately, most seeds and nuts can be harvested in season and stored for later use.

In other words, though nuts and berries comprise a very small percentage of available wild foods, and though they are available only seasonally, they are among the most essential plant foods that we need. It is no wonder that nuts and berries have been held in such high esteem for millennia by societies all over the world.

Edible, Medicinal, and Poisonous Plants

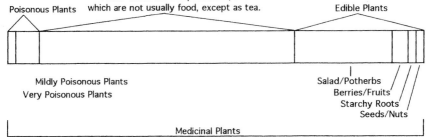

Thomas Elpel's chart is based on his years of observation and analysis and can be found in *Participating in Nature,* available from HOPS Press (www.hopspress.com). Elpel is also the author of *Botany in a Day.* Thomas Elpel

ENVIRONMENTAL REGIONS

The state of California is a complex place. Biology texts will show the state with lines delineating one biotic zone from another, and sometimes you can actually find clean and distinct biotic zones in nature. Studying these zones helps us to get an idea of the biological diversity of the state. But urban sprawl, farming, grazing, fires, and perhaps other factors have continued to blur the clean distinction of one zone to the other. Transition is everywhere, and many times plants choose to live outside the zone where we expect them to live. Thus, the categories listed below are the broad biological zones that you will find in California, with lots of overlap. These categories help you understand the state's biotic zones, but their borders are not hard and fast.

Desert—The largest desert in California is the Mojave Desert, which comprises a large portion of the southeastern part of the state. East of the Sierra Nevada, there's the Great Basin, and farther south, there's the Sonoran Desert. The desert is a region of limited precipitation and great temperature extremes. Plants have adapted to little water and constant winds. Plants typical of the desert regions include creosote bush, paloverde, mesquite, the native fan palm, and a vast variety of cacti.

Chaparral—Chaparral is a shrubland plant community that can be found from the ocean up to about 5,000 feet. It thrives in a Mediterranean climate (mild, wet winters and hot dry summers), and is subject to wildfire. Sometimes called the Upper Sonoran Zone, this plant community is found between the desert and the mountainous regions, consisting of such plants as laurel sumac, buckwheat, yucca, white sage, and other woody shrubs.

Ocean—The ocean zone is self-evident. Keep in mind that the interface between the ocean and the urban, chaparral, or mountain zones can be very short in distance, so plants from other environmental zones can be found on and near the beaches.

Mountain—The mountainous zones are higher elevations with typically colder temperatures, higher precipitation, and higher winds. Many plants prefer and need higher elevations and colder temperatures, and are often restricted to these areas.

Riparian—The riparian zone refers to the area along a river or stream, and around a lake. The plants in this zone require more water, and generally you won't find them far from water. The riparian regions are estimated to be between 1–2 percent of the total landscape, and some biologists say that the percentage is even less because more than 95 percent of California's riparian habitat has been lost.

Urban and Field—This includes the "urban sprawl." The plants found here are often considered "weeds." These plants do well in urban environment, valleys and fields, and at the edges of farms (such as throughout the Central Valley). Nearly all of these plants have come here from somewhere else, and they are nature's "survivors." They grow in lawns, backyards, cracks in the sidewalks, throughout all urban areas, and on the vast fringes of the urban sprawl. The plants we've listed in our HIPs section are largely found in urban backyards, though they often "escape" to the wild.

PLANT LISTING BY ENVIRONMENTAL SECTION

Some plants may be found in more than one section. Why? Because the plants do not read or abide by botanists' rules or definitions.

DESERT

Acorn
Elderberry
Ground cherry
Jojoba
Juniper

Mesquite
Palm date
Pine
Prickly pear

CHAPARRAL

Acorn
Bay nut
Blackberry
Buckeye
Cherry (wild)
Coffeeberry
Currant and gooseberry
Elderberry
Fig
Grape (wild)

Manzanita
Mulberry
Nightshade
Prickly pear
Rose hips (wild rose)
Sugar bush / lemonade berry /
  basket bush
Toyon
Walnut

OCEAN

Grape (wild)
Nightshade
Prickly pear

Sugar bush / lemonade berry /
  basket bush

MOUNTAIN

Acorn
Blackberry
Buckeye
Cherry (wild)
Chinquapin
Currants and gooseberries
Elderberry
Grape, (wild)
Huckleberry
Madrone

Manzanita
Nightshade
Oregon grape
Pine
Rose hips
Salal
Salmonberry
Serviceberry
Strawberry
Thimbleberry

RIPARIAN

Bay nuts
Blackberry

Grape (wild)
Rose hips

URBAN AND FIELD

Acorn
Blackberry
Cherry (wild)
Eugenia
Fig
Ginkgo
Grape (wild)
Jujube
Loquat
Mulberry

Natal plum
Nightshade
Olive
Oregon grape
Palm date
Pine
Prickly pear
Pyracantha
Rose hips
Walnut

LEAF ARRANGEMENTS, MARGINS, AND SHAPES

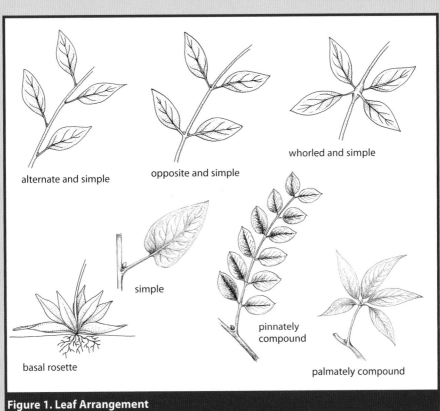

Figure 1. Leaf Arrangement

alternate and simple

opposite and simple

whorled and simple

simple

basal rosette

pinnately compound

palmately compound

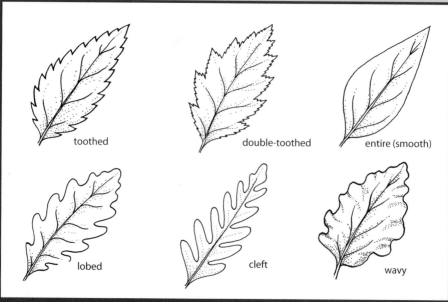

Figure 2. Leaf Margin

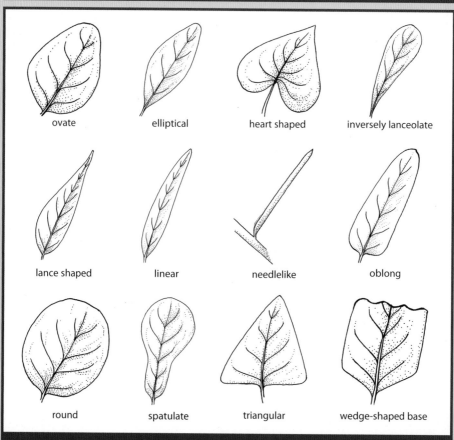

Figure 3. Leaf Shapes

NATIVES

Nuts

A live oak acorn

ACORN
Quercus spp. and *Notholithocarpus densiflorus*

Description: Acorns are the nuts of the oak tree. Each acorn has a scaly cap. Depending on the species of oak tree, each acorn is a bit different, and yet every child can recognize an acorn! Oak trees can be deciduous or evergreen, with some being bushes, though most are very large trees.

Uses: Acorns are leached of tannic acid and used to make pastry products.

Habitats: Oak trees are found widely in urban areas, in the chaparral, in the mountains, in the Central Valley. Their collective habitat is broad.

Range: There are 25 species of oak in the state, and they are widespread.

Tools: A bag or bucket is needed for collecting acorns. You need a hand stone to crack them open, and grinders and colanders, depending on how you'll be processing the acorns.

Acorns are produced by trees in the Oak family (Fagaceae). Worldwide, this family includes seven genera and about 900 species. There are three genera in California, and *Quercus* is the most widespread. There are twenty-five species of *Quercus* in California, not including the subspecies. Also included in this category is the tanbark oak or tanoak (*Notholithocarpus densiflorus*). This tree was once called *Quercus densiflora*, but has been reclassified into a different genus because of a few key differences. To the average person looking at the tanbark oak, it's very much an oak whose acorn caps appear "shaggy." Otherwise, the tanoak's acorn is used just like any other acorn. *Notholithocarpus* is one of the three genera of the Oak family in California, and the tanbark oak is the only species (with two varieties) of this genus. (The third genus of this family found in California is the chinquapin, which we deal with separately.)

Oak trees are everywhere in California, found in most environments. Most are large trees, but some are bushlike, such as the scrub oak. Some are evergreen (the "live" oaks), and some are deciduous, such as the black oak and valley oak. Oaks are inherently beautiful, and they convey a sense of the essence of what California is. They are perhaps the quintessential California tree, the source of food and survival for the indigenous peoples who lived here for millennia before the European invasion. The oak's very image expresses the stereotypical California landscape.

In the fall of most years, acorns drop from the trees, often in great numbers. Some years are better than others.

Acorns were so important to the indigenous California population that they could be regarded as the breadbasket in the pre-Spanish days. Nearly every California tribe used acorns. Acorns would be collected and stored, and then processed as needed. Acorns generally fall from the trees beginning in late September, and can still fall into January. It is best to collect the acorns off the ground so you know they are mature.

If you don't have the time to shell the acorns right away, you should dry them so they do not get moldy, and so that larvae does not develop. Lay them on cookie sheets in the full sun for a few days, or place them in an oven where a pilot light will help to dry them. When you're ready to begin cooking with acorns, your first step will be to shell them. If your acorns are dry, you can place each acorn on a flat rock, and hit it with another rock, and the shell will come off easily. You can try whatever works for you—a rock, a hammer, a piece of wood.

Then the acorns must be processed to remove the tannic acid, and there are several ways you can do this.

Let's look at the expedient way to process acorns first. Shell the acorns and put them into a pot. Cover with water and bring to a boil. Within a few minutes the water will look like mud, as the tannic acid comes out of the acorns. Dump the water and add fresh water. Bring to a boil again. Rinse, and do it again. How long do you do this? Since each variety of acorn has a different amount of tannic acid, you must periodically taste

---

BARBARA'S ACORN POUND CAKE

Mix together the following:

    ½ cup olive oil

    ¾ cup sugar or ½ cup honey

    2 eggs

    ½ cup acorn flour

Next, mix together the following:

    1¼ cups whole wheat flour

    ⅛ teaspoon salt

    ½ teaspoon cream of tartar

    ¼ teaspoon baking soda

Stir the second mixture into the first, a little at a time, alternating with the following:

    ¼ cup milk

    ½ teaspoon vanilla extract

    ¼ teaspoon mace or ½ teaspoon nutmeg

Beat the mixture all well. Pour into an oiled 8-inch square or round pan, or a bread pan. Bake at 350 degrees for 50 to 60 minutes.

---

one of the acorns. Still bitter? OK, do another boiling. When you taste the acorn and it's just bland, with no bitterness, it should be done.

When the acorns are leached, you could actually just toss them in a pot with vegetables and seasonings, and make a stew. Or, if you're out camping, you might mash up the leached acorns on a rock, and use the mush as a thickener for a soup or stew.

If you're at home and you try this method, you could also run the acorns through a meat grinder to reduce them to a coarse meal, and then process them into a finer meal, as needed.

You could also try processing the acorns using a method that is more akin to the way it was done by the indigenous peoples of California, the method that I prefer.

First the acorns are shelled, and then I grind them on a flat metate, as was done in the old days. Next, I line a colander with a piece of cotton, and put in the ground acorn meal. I then pour cold water through the acorn meal, and let it filter through the cotton, taking the tannic acid out with it. It will likely take several pourings to get out all the bitterness.

The time required to leach the acorns is partly a factor of how bitter the acorns are in the first place, which is determined by species. It's also a factor of what sort of cotton you use for the filter. Don't use a tight-weave cotton fabric, like a pillowcase, since it will take too long for the water to filter through. You should use something like a cotton kerchief.

I like to make pancakes, biscuits, or cookies with acorns. For pancakes or biscuits, I use 50 percent acorn flour to 50 percent whole wheat or mixed grain flour. I add more water to the pancake batter, and less to the biscuit mix. For cookies, I use the same blend, often adding raisins or peanut butter.

Harvested black walnuts in bowl. Note the thick shell.

BLACK WALNUT
(Juglans californica and *J. hindsii)*

The black walnut is a member of the Walnut family (Juglandaceae). The Walnut family contains nine genera and about sixty species worldwide. In California, it is represented by the *Carya* genus (the pecan), and the *Juglans* genus. In California, there are two native species of *Juglans*, as well as the introduced English walnut.

Description: The black walnut is widespread in California in canyons, valleys, and on hillsides. The two species that might be encountered are *J. californica*, the Southern California black walnut, and *J. hindsii*, the Northern California black walnut. Additionally, you may encounter the English walnut (*J. regia*), either planted in yards or surviving around old farms and cabins.

The California walnut is a full-bodied, native, deciduous tree with pinnately divided leaves. There are typically from eleven to nineteen leaflets per leaf. Black walnuts have a soft, green, outer layer, which turns black as it matures and has long been used as a dye. The black walnut is nearly half shell, and it requires a rock

WALNUT TREAT

Collect about three dozen black walnuts, and carefully crack them open with a rock or hammer. Carefully pick out the meat. You won't end up with a lot of walnut meat, but it's very tasty. Roast at a low temperature for half an hour. (If you're not going to use the nuts right away, let them dry thoroughly in the oven. Then pack in jars.) These are likely to be small pieces already, but if not, chop them coarsely. Toss them on vanilla ice cream and enjoy.

or a hammer to crack. The meat in the black walnut is oily and delicious, though there's not as much meat as you'd find in the cultivated English walnut.

Uses: The wild black walnuts are eaten and used in recipes in just the same way as the common English walnut is used.

Habitats: Black walnuts are common at lower elevations in canyons and valleys.

Range: *J. Californica* is widespread in Southern California, along the coast and in the transverse ranges, and into the Central Valley. *J. hindsii* is mostly found in the central part of the state and is on the California Native Plant Society Inventory of Rare and Endangered Plants.

Tools: When collecting black walnuts, bring along a bag or box, and be sure to wear gloves. When cracking them, you'll need a hammer or some rocks.

California's black walnuts are very much like the hickory nuts found in the eastern states: They are mostly shell, and perhaps less than half nut meat. They mature and fall from the trees in September.

As the nuts begin their development, they are covered with a green outer layer. This layer matures into a mushy texture and turns black. This black outer layer is also a very good dye, so you should wear gloves if you are collecting the nuts while the outer layer is still "wet." You can also just collect after the walnuts have dried.

Forager Notes: Green, immature black walnuts were once crushed and tossed into pools of water by the indigenous Californians to stun the fish. Then, the fish would be scooped out by hand or with nets.

Green walnuts in the tree. Note the leaf pattern.

You will need to crack open the nuts with a rock or a hammer. If you crack the nut from the top, you're more likely to get an even split, which will make it easier to extract the meat.

Even then, a little nut pick will be handy for separating out the shell from the meat. It could take a while to get enough walnuts for a cake, cookie, or other dessert item.

The meat of walnuts was widely used by all the Native American tribes who had access to it. Sometimes it was mixed with other seeds and berries to make a type of bread. The nut meats were added to various soups, such as corn soup. Sometimes, the nut meats were crushed, boiled, and the oil allowed to come to the top. The walnut oil was then used for various recipes.

Immature bay nuts in the tree

CALIFORNIA BAY
(Umbellularia californica)

California bay is a member of the Laurel family (Lauraceae). The Laurel family has fifty-four genera and 3,500 species worldwide. In California, it is only represented by the camphor tree (*Cinnamomum camphora*) and the California bay.

Description: This is an evergreen tree usually found along streams. The bark is smooth, and the leaves are shiny green and lanceolate. When you scratch the bark or crush the leaves, you smell the strong characteristic odor.

Uses: The nuts are used for food, and the leaves are used for seasoning sauces and soups. The long straight branches make good archery bows.

Habitats: The California bay tree is primarily found in riparian environments. However, it is easily planted and can sometimes be found in urban areas as a yard or street tree.

Range: The natural range is in the riparian areas from California south into Baja California.

Tools: A bag is needed for collecting the nuts, usually off the ground.

A selection of gathered bay nuts. Dark-skinned nuts are the most mature.

Bay trees are found along the rivers from the Central part of the state, south into Baja. As far as I know, they are not found in the wild outside of this area. But since the bay tree is easily cultivated, it's possible to find some grown as park trees and hedges outside of its native zone.

The tree is an attractive evergreen with stiff, lanceolate leaves. There are no overtly attractive flowers and the bark is smooth, not unlike the bark of the young alders that also line the streams. Occasionally you might step on some leaves and a pungent aroma will fill the air. You've found the bay tree. When you take a fresh leaf, it will feel stiff and almost waxy. Crush it in your hand and the strong fragrance will be exposed. You should be able to identify the tree simply by the odor of the crushed leaf.

The plant flowers, and by late summer to fall, produces green fruits, which mature into a dark fruit. The mature fruit consists of a wrinkly outer flesh layer, and then a thin shell. Inside is the edible portion, which is usually not eaten raw, but dried or cooked.

The fruits ripen in October and into November. You can pick them off the tree or the ground. Before fully mature, the fleshy outer layer is green, but that matures into a mushy outer layer, turning brown and appearing wrinkled. After you collect, you remove the outer layer.

The nut has a thin shell that is easily cracked. You should taste the meat inside, which is usually a bit strong for most palates. The raw flavor is a mix of astringency and slight bitterness, along with its unique flavor. There are various ways to prepare the nut for food.

I have always preferred to shell the nut, and then to bake it. It can then be served as a snack, if you like it plain. It could be salted, or seasoned with other spices. Simple!

BAY NUTS: TWO METHODS OF PREPARATION, PROVIDED BY PAUL CAMPBELL

1. With the shell hard, I dry and keep the nuts this way, sometimes for many years. To dry the fresh nuts, place in a cast-iron pan and start in an oven at 200 degrees. After fifteen minutes, go to 250 degrees, at thirty minutes to 300 degrees, and at one hour to 330 (the slow process avoids an explosion you can't believe) until the kernel itself is dark. Broken open, it becomes a rich, delicious food for many of us.

2. Sometimes Indians gathered the bay kernels, roasted them, and ground them into an oily meal in a mortar. The meal was pressed and molded into flat cakes 2 inches in diameter by 1 inch thick, set in the sun, and dried for the winter.

Cakes or nuts were often eaten by the Pomo as a condiment, with clover or other greens, or with buckeye meal, acorn bread, mush, or even seaweed. The Yuki used the nuts for long, forced journeys through the woods or when without standard food.

Paul Campbell, author of *Survival Skills of Native California*, has a unique way of preparing the nuts. He shells and then bakes the nuts until they are almost—but not quite —burned. The flavor is oddly reminiscent of chocolate! Still, it seems to be a bit of an acquired taste. Some people love them and I've seen others spit them out!

Bay nuts are typically used as a snack food, though they could be ground up into a flour and added to breads, biscuits, pancakes.

These fruits were widely used by the Native Americans of California. The nuts were said to have been eaten raw, but most were dried and roasted first. They were also ground into a flour and stored for later use. Sometimes, this flour would be formed into cakes and dried for later use.

The leaves of the California bay can be used in all the traditional ways of using European bay, such as adding to soups, stews, and sauces for Italian dishes. The leaves can be used fresh or dry, and fresh is much stronger. One leaf in a cup of cold or hot water will make a delicious beverage. However, if you're making a cold beverage, you should break up the leaf into the water and let it sit for a while.

The buckeye seed in the tree with the husk cracking open

CALIFORNIA BUCKEYE
(Aesculus californica)

California buckeye was formerly classified as a member of Hippocastanaceae, or the Buckeye family. However, it is now classified as part of the Soapberry family (Sapindaceae). This family includes 150 genera and 1,500 species worldwide.
In California, there are only two genera of the Soapberry family, which are *Acer* (Maple) and *Aesculus* (buckeye).

There are about fifteen species of *Aesculus* in the Northern Hemisphere, though California buckeye is the only species represented in the wild in California. (Some may be cultivated.)

Description: This is a large shrub or a small tree, deciduous, with palmately divided leaves divided into five to seven segments. The seeds are large, about 2 inches across, dark brown, and shiny.

Uses: The seeds were eaten by Northern California Indians, and also used as a fish toxin.

Habitats: Typically found along the borders of streams, in canyons, on dry slopes, and generally scattered in the foothills

Range: Less common in Southern California, and more common north of San Francisco, in mostly the western part of the state

Tools: None required

Whoa! Are buckeye nuts even edible? Don't they contain a poison? Indeed they do, which is why one of their most popular uses in the old days was to crush the fresh nuts and toss them into pools of water so that fish would be stunned. The fish would float to the top of the water and would be scooped out by hand or with nets.

The poison in the buckeye is water-soluble, so processing in a manner similar to acorns is sufficient to make them edible.

According to records from the contact of early explorers with the indigenous peoples of California, and according to traditions among the tribes, it appears that the use of buckeyes for food was never as popular as the use of acorns, and use of buckeyes may have been very limited. There were apparently several variations for rendering the nuts edible. The Miwok were said to have used buckeyes for food only when the acorn crop failed.

I spoke to Dr. James Adams about the processing of the buckeye fruits for food. Dr. Adams, who is a doctor of pharmacology at the University of Southern California, explained that it may be very difficult to make buckeye nuts taste good. Dr. Adams suggested adding toyon berries, elderberries, blackberries, or some other fruit to improve the flavor.

He further explained that buckeye nuts contain several toxic compounds that are all water-soluble. "There are several methods for extracting the toxins," according to Dr. Adams. Here is what he suggests:

1. Break the nuts open, soak in water for a day, pound the nuts into a meal, leach the meal ten times, boil, and eat. Leaching involves pouring water onto the meal, allowing the water to percolate through until the meal dries and cracks.
2. Pound the nut into a meal, leach ten times, boil, and eat. This usually involves eight to ten hours of leaching.

3. Leach the buckeye meal for several weeks, until it is white and odorless, before boiling and eating.
4. Cook the nuts for ten hours in a stone-lined oven covered with ash, mash the nuts into a meal, then leach the meal for several days before eating.
5. Boil the nuts, mash them, and leach them before eating.

I shared with Dr. Adams that when I eat buckeye, I boil the nuts with ten changes of water. He responded, "Your method of producing a meal and boiling in ten changes of water sounds good to me. [. . .] The main concern is to produce a fine meal that can be thoroughly leached. The correctly prepared meal is described as 'not as palatable as acorn meal.' This was a survival food that was eaten only when there were not enough acorns. I encourage you to keep trying with buckeye. Adding buckwheat, pinyon nuts, or other foods may help the flavor."

What exactly is the toxin in our buckeye nuts? After doing considerable research in books and on the Internet, I again spoke with Dr. James Adams. Here is how he responded:

"All the information available on the Internet about buckeye is wrong and uses information from other *Aesculus* species. There are four papers published on the chemicals in buckeye. A paper just published in 2013 found fifteen new compounds called aesculiosides. These are saponins and are found in the husks, not the nuts. A paper from 1992 found arbutin in the nut and epicatechin in the seed coat. A paper from 1968 found an unusual amino acid in the nuts, 2-amino-4-methylhex-4-enoic acid. Arbutin is not toxic and is used as a skin care product, although there have been questions about whether it might cause cancer. The possible toxic component of the nuts is 2-amino-4-methylhex-4-enoic acid. Nothing is known about the toxicity of this compound. We know the

> **Forager Notes:** The wood of the buckeye makes a good fire hearth for making a fire with a hand drill or with the bow and drill. This wood was one of Ishi's favorites.

COOKING AND RECIPES—POMO METHOD

The following details come from Karen Adams, a Dry Creek Pomo who shared how her cousin and mother processed buckeye seeds.

Her cousin, Dorothy Duncan, who is now in her late 70s, was born on the rancheria. Dorothy said to gather the buckeye seeds when the brown outer husk is just starting to split. She added that she and her mother would always try to get the biggest buckeye seeds, the ones that were about the size of small oranges.

When ready to eat, Dorothy would boil the buckeyes for about five minutes, and then change the water. The outer husk would be taken off as the seeds got soft.

Boiling and changing the water would be repeated about five times, until the buckeye nuts had the consistency of boiled potatoes. She would keep another kettle of hot water ready to add to the buckeye after each changing of the water so the process would take less time.

After the boiling, Dorothy would mash the buckeyes, and eat them with salt and pepper. Without that seasoning, it was described as having no flavor, and since the processed buckeye were said to not complement other foods (in the way that acorns did), it was not used that often.

Karen Adams's mother would do the same boiling and changing of the water until the buckeyes was the consistency of boiled potatoes. Then her mother would mash the buckeye, refrigerate it, and then would serve with sugar and vanilla. "It was served like a dessert," said Karen.

nuts are toxic to fish. It is possible that the amino acid is the toxic agent. This needs to be tested. The amino acid is water soluble and will be extracted by leaching."

A view of chinquapin leaf and fruit Photo by Julie Kierstead Nelson

CHINQUAPIN
(Chrysolepis spp.*)*

Chinquapins are a member of the Oak family (Fagaceae). Worldwide, this family includes seven genera and about 900 species. There are three genera in California, and *Quercus* is the most widespread (see Acorn, page 2). The second genus is *Notholithocarpus*, of which there is only one species, *N. densiflorus*, or tanbark oak, which is treated in the Acorn chapter.

The third genus of the Oak family is *Chrysolepis*, or chinquapin, of which there are two species. The giant chinquapin, (*C. chrysophylla*), is the most common, with two varieties. The second species is bush chinquapin (*C. sempervirens*).

Description: An evergreen tree or shrub with leathery leaves, oblong to lanceolate. The margins are entire or slightly wavy. The fruit is burrlike, spiny, and enclosing one to three ovoid nuts.

Uses: The nuts are edible.

Habitats: Chinquapin is found in open woods at lower elevations.

Range: The plant is found throughout California in the mountainous regions, and is more common in the northern part of the state. It can be found into Oregon and Washington.

Tools: A bag is needed for collecting.

Though chinquapin is related to the oak trees, the fruits don't look like acorns. Rather, the fruits look like a sycamore tree bur, but a bit bigger. The nuts don't need to be leached, which can save a lot of time. Once the nuts are removed from the spiny bur, you will find one to three nuts per cluster. These can be eaten raw, and are improved by roasting.

The nuts were widely used by the Indians of California, mostly in the northern part of the state. Sometimes they were simply eaten when scouts or hunters were in the field, as reported about the Kawaiisu.

The Karok roasted these nuts and ate them, and also stored them for the winter. The Pomo also stored them for winter use, usually while left in the shell. In general, the chinquapin nut was used in the past as a trail snack, eaten as is, roasted and eaten, ground into a meal and added to other foods, or stored for winter use.

Though widely used, it was not as abundant as the far more widely used acorns.

CHINQUAPIN NUT MIX

Collect the small nuts of the chinquapin and mix with chopped walnuts, filberts, and Brazil nuts in equal amounts. Carry as a trail nut mix or serve at parties as a side dish.

The jojoba plant in flower

JOJOBA
(Simmondsia chinensis)

Jojoba (pronounced hoe-hoe-buh) is a member of the Jojoba family (Simmondsia-ceae). There is one genus in the Jojoba family, and only one species to this genus, which is *S. chinensis*. That means botanists have found this plant to be unique!

Description: The shrub has smooth bark and opposite leaves that are leathery, ovate, and dull green. The nutlike fruit is obtusely three-sided.

Uses: The nuts are used for food.

Habitats: The plant is found in the low desert and on sandy flats.

Range: This evergreen shrub is found throughout the entire Southwest and into Mexico, especially in arid areas and washes.

Tools: A bag for collecting the nuts

I have long eaten jojoba nuts from the desert as a snack or nibble, usually raw, but sometimes baked. When a friend first saw me eating some, she said with alarm, "You can't do that! They make car wax out of those nuts!"

Yes, it's true that there are many industrial uses for the jojoba, but it's also a fact that desert Indians have eaten the nuts for generations.

I was first exposed to this desert seed when visiting my friend Nathaniel Schleimer, who once worked for the National Park Service in the Anza Borrego region, where jojoba was common. We never made a meal out of these nuts, but supplemented other foods with them, and used them sparingly as a snack. We found them tasty, oily, nutty, and very appealing. Though we often ate them raw, we preferred them dried or roasted.

Jojoba nuts were eaten fresh or dried by desert Indians. According to Garcia and Adams, authors of *Healing with Medicinal Plants of the West*, "It is not recommended to eat the nuts in large amounts, since they may cause anemia. It is not known if roasting or boiling destroys the simmondsins in the nuts. Therefore, it is not recommended to eat the roasted or boiled nuts in large amounts."

The Cahuilla, who lived in the greater desert area surrounding modern Palm Springs, ate jojoba nuts raw or ground them into a flour that was used to make a coffeelike beverage. Other desert tribes either ground the nuts and used them as a flour, or used them as a trail nibble.

I collect all the jojoba nuts that I can if I'm around the stands of the plant when the nuts are ripe. I enjoy them as a snack. Typically, I let them dry naturally, and then eat them. Sometimes, I'll roast them first.

PALM DESERT SNACK
Soak the nuts in a mixture of 50 percent water and 50 percent quality soy sauce. Drain, then roast. Serve as a snack or side dish.

Mesquite pods in a molcajete, ready for grinding

MESQUITE PODS AND SCREWBEANS
Prosopis glandulosa and *P. pubescens*

Mesquite and screwbean are a part of the Legume family (Fabaceae). This is a big family worldwide, with about 730 genera and 19,400 species. In California, this large group is represented by fifty genera. There are forty-four species of *Prosopis* worldwide, with three found in California.

Description: Mesquite grows as bushes or small trees. The leaf is evenly and pinnately divided into smaller round or linear segments, giving the plant a ferny look. There are little spines on the stems, generally two per node. The mesquite fruits, which appear in the summer, are pale yellow, dry, and maybe 6 inches long. They look like slightly withered green beans, but yellow. The screwbean plant is hard to tell from the mesquite when not in fruit, but the screwbean pods looks distinctly different from the yellow bean mesquite pod; screwbean looks like a rounded bean that is spiral-twisted.

Uses: The pods are used for food.

Habitat: Mesquite is found in the desert.

A view of the mesquite branch, with leaf and flower   Photo by Rick Adams

Range: Mesquite and screwbean are most common in the lower desert regions, with mesquite being much more common.

Tools: None are needed, except a bag

Mesquite is very common throughout the low desert, and its close relative, the screwbean, is not so common. You've driven past mesquite if you've been around Palm Springs. If the plant wasn't in flower or fruit, it's somewhat inconspicuous and you may not have known it was mesquite.

When not in flower or fruit, the two trees are very hard to discern. But when in fruit, the screwbean is just as the name implies, a bean that looks like you twisted it. It's somewhat shorter than the mesquite fruit, and round in cross section.

The yellow pods of mesquite are the main prize of this desert shrub or tree. They are harvested when ripe, which is typically sometime in the summer. There are a number of ways in which the pods have been used for food over the centuries. Perhaps one of the simplest is to just pick a mature pod, chew it, and spit out the seeds. (The screwbean pod is used similarly.)

In traditional diets, the entire pod—seed and all—would be ground into a flour, which was then used in various recipes. The flour can be used alone, or can be mixed with other flours to make breads or cakes.

In *Foraging California,* we describe an excellent meal that can be made from the mesquite pods.

Recently, when I visited Paul Campbell (author of *Survival Skills of Native California*), he served me a drink and asked me to guess what I was drinking. I took a slow sip of the very sweet, warm drink. It turned out that he simply brewed some pounded mesquite meal in hot water, and poured off the dark liquid into my cup. It was absolutely delicious, one that even the most finicky and discriminating eaters will rave about.

MESQUITE BEAN CAKE

Paul Campbell mixes ground, whole-bean, dried mesquite flour into boiling water. He then reduces the heat and blends it into a thick mush. He simmers and stirs a few minutes longer to tenderize (especially if the flour is coarse), and then he blends in additional flour until the mixture thickens and stiffens enough to hold shape. Campbell then spreads this mixture as cakes 2 to 4 inches in diameter and about ½-inch thick on a cookie sheet or on tinfoil, and dries the cakes in sun or on rocks near fire.

These rich cakes, with a molasses-like flavor, were travel food for California desert Indians. After preparation, pieces were broken off and eaten, or reconstituted in water to make a hot or cold drink.

Pine nuts on a stone, ready to be shelled

PINE NUTS
Pinus spp.

The Pine family consists of ten genera and 193 species. One genus is *Pinus*, of which there are ninety-four species in the Northern Hemisphere. Not counting subspecies, there are nineteen species of *Pinus* in California.

Description: Pines are one of the easier conifers to identify because all of the needles are "bundled" at their base into groups of one to five, with papery sheaths called fascicles. There is a fascicle at the base of the needle even when there is only one needle, as in one of the pinyons.

The pines in California range from short bushes to large, towering trees. Their seeds are produced in cones, which are often whorled with a variety of scale types. As the cones mature, they open up to reveal a pine nut under each scale. Each pine nut has a thin black shell and a white oily seed inside.

Uses: The harvested nuts are eaten raw or cooked; the needles are used for tea and spice.

Habitats: Various species are found in the mountains or desert regions. Pines are often planted in urban areas.

Range: Pines are widespread throughout the state. Some are found in higher elevations and some are found in the deserts. Some have been widely planted along city streets, in parks, and in yards.

Tools: No special tools are required to collect pine nuts—just a bag.

In theory, every pine nut is edible. Yes, none are toxic, and all can be eaten. But in practice, some are very small, and some are difficult to harvest. Some may be too bitter to eat. Most people who harvest pine nuts go after the very best ones, such as the pinyon.

First, make sure you're looking at a pine tree. All conifers have cones, and all conifers have needles, but not all cones will yield useful nuts.

Most nonpine conifers have single needles, whereas the pines have bundled needles, with a papery sheath (called a fascicle) at the base, bundling the needles together. Even the single-needled pinyon pine has a fascicle, so you can look at the needles closely and immediately know if you have a pine or not.

PINYON NUT SOUP

Begin with a quart of milk and two cups of water. Yes, you can substitute almond milk or rice milk for cow's milk, and the flavor will be different. Add a pound of raw pine nuts. Some people puree the pine nuts, and others leave them whole. I leave them whole. You're not going to boil this, but rather just bring it to a simmer, and then keep it on low heat for about half an hour.

If you choose to add some seasoning, do it at the very beginning. Some common spices can be used in pinyon soup: Add what you like. For this recipe, you can try five diced green onions; a few coriander seeds; a few mint leaves; or ½ cup or so of chicken broth.

Once the soup has cooked for about half an hour, you can serve it. It's delicious and rich.

Pinyon pine needles

The pine nuts are found at the base of each scale, and they fall out when the cone opens. They have a thin black shell and a white, meaty inside. The seeds drop out around October.

The pine nuts were used by Chumash, Gabrielino/Tongva, and probably every tribe who had these growing in their areas.

I have long heard that if an Indian child's mother died or was killed, others could make a mother's milk substitute by mashing and diluting pine nuts. The nuts seem to be most nutritious, though I don't know if this was really a widespread practice. Still, it elicited the idea that I could actually eat from the breast of the Earth Mother by eating the pine nut! Pine nuts can be mixed with raisins for a trail snack, or added to many other cooked dishes, such as rice, soups, stews, even salads.

Berries

Farm-grown blackberries

THE *RUBUS* BROTHERS
Blackberries and Raspberries
Rubus spp.

Blackberries and raspberries are members of the Rose family (Rosaceae). The Rose family contains 110 genera and 3,000 species worldwide. Species from forty-five of the genera are found in California. Blackberries and raspberries belong to the *Rubus* genus, and there are 400 to 750 species of *Rubus* worldwide. There are eleven species of *Rubus* in California (not including varieties).

The *Rubus* species consist of the following:

Natives

California blackberry (*R. ursinus*)

Waxleaf raspberry (*R. glaucifolius*)

Roughfruit raspberry (*R. lasiococcus*)

Whitebark raspberry (*R. leucodermis*)

Snow dwarf bramble (*R. nivalis*)

Thimbleberry (*R. parviflorus*) [See full treatment on page 31]

Salmonberry (*R. spectabilis*) [See full treatment on page 30]

Exotics

Himalayan blackberry (*R. armeniacus*)

Cutleaf blackberry (*R. laciniatus*)

Elmleaf blackberry (*R. ulmifolius*)

No common name (*R. pensilvanicus*)

Description: The leaves of blackberries and raspberries are palmately divided (like a hand) into three, five, or seven segments. The vines are twining on the ground or over low hedges, and are characterized by their thorns, which makes it difficult to wade too deep into any of the old hedgelike stands of wild blackberries. The flowers are white and five-petaled, and are followed by the fruits, which are aggregate fruits. Most people instantly recognize the shape of the blackberry because they've seen it in the supermarket or in the backyard garden. The aggregate fruit is a collection of sweet drupelets, with the fruit separating from the flower stalk to form a somewhat hollow, thimblelike shape.

Uses: The ripe fruits are eaten fresh, or made into a variety of jams, jellies, and juices. The leaves are sometimes used medicinally. Made into an infusion, the leaf tea can be used to treat cases of mild diarrhea. Gargling with an infusion of blackberry leaf is also good for mouth irritations, such as bleeding gums or sore throat.

Habitats: The *Rubus* species and their kin are fairly widespread and distributed throughout the state. These vines are at home growing in high elevations, in chaparral, along dusty trails, along streams, near the beach . . . everywhere!

Range: Blackberries and raspberries prefer areas where sufficient water is supplied. They have also been widely planted, and survive well in diverse places.

Tools: Gloves and clippers can be a good idea when harvesting ripe blackberries. You should also bring shallow baskets that can be stacked, so that the fragile fruits do not get crushed.

Everyone recognizes blackberries, don't they? Blackberries are found all over the world, and are widely recognized for their edible berries. The plant is a sprawling vine full of thorns. The leaves are typically divided into three leaflets, but you can also find five or seven leaflets. Sometimes people confuse poison oak with blackberry vines, but poison oak lacks the spines. In the spring, blackberry vines are full of the five-petaled white flowers, the ovary of which develops into the characteristic aggregate fruit by early to midsummer.

The fruits are aggregate fruits, which seem to be universally recognized. Very few people hesitate when they see a ripe blackberry.

California blackberries (*Rubus ursinus*) were eaten fresh, and dried for winter use, by the Pomo, Bear River, Cahuilla, northern Diegueño, and other native Californians. Sometimes the Cahuilla would collect the half-ripe berries and soak them in water to make what would have been a lemonade-type drink. Many other groups used the blackberries for food, including the Salinan, Chumash, and Gabrielino/Tongva.

The California blackberry (*Rubus vitifolius*) were eaten fresh, and also dried for winter, by the Karok, Hupa, Miwok, Salinan, Cahuilla, Luiseño, and other California tribes.

Forager Notes: According to Gregory Tilford, an herbalist who authored *Edible and Medicinal Plants of the West*, both the leaves and flowers of these species can be used as an infusion, both because of their flavor and their vitamin and mineral content. Tilford describes this as a "female tonic," which is effective probably because of the plant's fragrene content, which is a substance believed to tone the body's smooth muscle organs. Tilford cautions that you should only use the fresh or completely dry leaves for this infusion.

The raspberry (*Rubus leucodermis*) was used in the same manner as the blackberry by native people throughout the state.

Fruits of all these varieties were used fresh, sun dried, in jams and jellies, in puddings, mixed with other nuts and berries for various dishes, as a sweetener, as a juice, in pies, etc.

Salmonberries
(Rubus spectabilis)

Salmonberry is a member of the Rose family (Rosaceae), which contains 110 genera and 3,000 species worldwide. Species from forty-five of the genera are found in California. Salmonberries, as well as blackberries and raspberries, belong to the *Rubus* genus. There are 400 to 750 species of *Rubus* worldwide. There are eleven species of *Rubus* in California (not including varieties), which include blackberry, raspberry, and thimbleberry.

Description: This is a native spiny vine, much like other members of this genus, and salmonberry often forms dense thickets. The stems are erect, or arching over, with a reddish-brown color. Leaves are alternate, trifoliate, with irregular teeth

Salmonberry in the field Photo by Vernon Smith

on the margins. The terminal leaflet is the largest. The showy flowers are reddish purple, generally solitary, about 1 inch across. The base of the flower (hypanthium) is bowl-shaped. The aggregate fruits are typical of the *Rubus* genus, in this case composed of salmon to dark-red drupelets. They look pretty much like a raspberry.

Uses: The fruits are edible.

Habitats: Found in mountainous areas, generally at the higher elevations such as subalpine meadows

Range: Salmonberries are mostly found from approximately San Francisco northward (and into the Northwest), in the mountainous regions along the coast.

Tools: None (though wearing long sleeves will help)

Many of the northern California native peoples ate salmonberries fresh from the bush. The Pomo ate them, and so did the Bear River Band. In fact, all the species of *Rubus* produce edible berries that are excellent when made into jams, jellies, pies, or preserves. At least twenty species of *Rubus* are known to grow in western North America. I'd suggest reading the section on the uses of the blackberries (page 28) because everything that's said about the uses of blackberry is applicable to the salmonberry.

Though each of the *Rubus* berries are slightly different, recipes for blackberries, raspberries, and thimbleberries are interchangeable.

Thimbleberries
Rubus parviflorus

Thimbleberries are members of the Rose family (Rosaceae), which contains 110 genera and 3,000 species worldwide. Species from forty-five of the genera are found in California. Thimbleberries belong to the *Rubus* genus. There are 400 to 750 species of *Rubus* worldwide; eleven of those species occur in California (not including varieties).

Description: *Rubus parviflorus* is a dense shrub that can grow up to 6 or 7 feet tall. Whereas most members of *Rubus* have prickles, the thimbleberry has no prickles on the stems. The large, five-lobed leaves are palmate, measuring up to about 8 inches across. The leaves are soft and fuzzy. The flowers consist of five white petals and numerous light yellow stamens. The flowers measure up to about 2½ inches across, which makes this one of the largest of the *Rubus* genus. The aggregate fruit

Thimbleberry fruit Photo by Aaron Arthur

is typical of *Rubus*, and will appear as a blackberry or raspberry. The fruit ripens to a bright red by the middle of the summer. Like other members of this group, the drupelets can be picked off the core, which leaves a hollow fruit with the appearance of a thimble. This is the source of the plant's common name.

Uses: Fruits are eaten raw, dried, or made into jams.

Habitats: Thimbleberry grows throughout the state, and can be found at higher elevations in the southern part of the state. This species typically grows along roadsides, railroad tracks, and in forest clearings, sometimes appearing as fire follower.

Range: Throughout the state

Tools: A box or basket for gathering

Look at the Latin name of thimbleberry: It tells you that it's in the same genus as all the blackberries. Except the thimbleberry is somewhat upright, not a sprawling-all-over-the-place thorny vine like the blackberry.

Thimbleberries were widely used by native peoples in California, such as the Cahuilla, Luiseño, Karok, Pomo, Bear River, Hupa, Yokut, and others. They were used generally in the same manner as blackberries and raspberries.

The fruits are great just eaten raw as a trail nibble. They can be easily dried for later use.

The thimbleberry fruits are a bit larger and softer than blackberries. Because of the softness, the fruit doesn't pack or ship too well, so thimbleberries are not readily available commercially. Plus, the fruit is usually somewhat scant, making commercial production a problem.

Many parts of the *Rubus parviflorus* plant were used for a great variety of medicinal purposes by Native Americans. Both the sprout of the plants and the fruits are high in vitamin C. The leaves were made into an infusion to treat vomiting. Dried and powdered thimbleberry leaves have been sprinkled into wounds and onto burns to reduce scars and promote healing. Chewing on dried thimbleberry leaves is said to relieve a stomachache, and even diarrhea, according to Nancy Turner and Marcus Bell, authors of "The Ethnobotany of the Coast Salish Indians of Vancouver Island" published in the journal *Economic Botany* in 1971.

Ripe wild cherries

CHERRY (WILD)
Prunus spp.

Wild cherries are members of the Rose family (Rosaceae), which contains 110 genera and 3,000 species worldwide. Species from forty-five of the genera are found in California.

Wild cherries are members of the *Prunus* genus, of which there are about 400 species worldwide. There are eleven species of *Prunus* in California, including cherry, almond, apricot, and plum, but we're only concerned with the cherries here.

The four wild cherries in California are:

- Hollyleaf cherry (*Prunus ilicifolia*, subspecies *ilicifolia*)
- Catalina Island cherry (*Prunus ilicifolia*, subspecies *lyonii*)
- Bitter cherry (*P. emarginata*)
- Western chokecherry (*P. virginiana* var. *demissa*)

The first two are sometimes also known as wild plums. *P. virginiana* also known as chokecherry.

Description: The first two wild cherries listed above are evergreen trees or bushes in California. The leaves are stiff and shiny, with teeth on the margins (depending on species). Bitter cherry and western chokecherry are deciduous.

One way to identify the plant is to crush the leaves, wait a few seconds, and then smell them. They will have a distinct aroma of bitter almond extract, your clue that the leaf contains cyanide (hydrocyanic acid). The fruits are very much like cultivated cherries, except the color is darker red, almost maroon, sometimes even darker. The flesh layer can be very thin in dry years, and thicker in the seasons following a good rain. Like domestic cherries, there is a thin shell around the meaty inside of the seed.

Uses: The flesh of the fruit is used in jams and jellies, and even cough syrup; the meat of the large seed can be processed into a flour.

Habitats: Chaparral, coastal ranges, riparian zones, urban fringes

Range: Wild cherries can be found widely throughout the state, often growing in urban vacant lots and hedgerows.

Tools: You don't need any special tools to collect cherries, just a bag or box.

Wild cherries are very common throughout the state. Though largely found throughout the chaparral (and related) regions, the wild cherry is also somewhat common in urban areas. The trees can sometimes grow large, but are typically bushes, sometimes tall.

The evergreen varieties produce their fruit most abundantly in August. The leaves are typically shiny, dark green, with few to many pointed edges, depending on the variety.

The tree develops clusters of the creamy-white flowers in the spring, and the green fruits begin to develop in early summer. By about August (depending on the location, weather, amount of rain, etc.), the fruits mature to a color that ranges from a pink tone to a deep dark red.

You can pick the fruits and eat the flesh for a trail snack. If ripe and if it was a wet winter, they're sweet and succulent. After dry winters, the flesh is thin, somewhat dry, and a bit tart. The fruits can be cooked and the seeds removed. The pulp of the fruit can be made into jams or preserves, and even used as a tasty and traditional cough syrup. My favorite is fruit leather, made by spreading the slightly cooked fruit pulp onto cookie sheets and laying it in the sun until dry.

Native Americans ate the fruit fresh, and sometimes mixed with meat. Also, the seed ("pit") was considered an important food source. The Chumash, for example, were primarily interested in the kernels of the cherries and had to process them to remove the hydrocyanic acid.

The seeds would be shelled and the meat removed. The inside is then boiled, and the water changed. One boiling might be sufficient with older seeds, but I always change the water at least twice just to be safe. Then, you can taste the seeds. They have a sweet, nutty flavor. You can mash or grind these seeds and add to soup for a sweet gravy. Or you can dry and grind the seeds into a flour, and then mix the flour about 50/50 with other flour for breads, biscuits, or pancakes.

According to Dr. James Adams, coauthor of *Healing with Medicinal Plants of the West*, "The food that was preferred to acorns was hollyleaf cherry pits. The pits require proper preparation (chop up the inside of the seed, pour several boilings of water over it to remove the cyanide) to avoid dying from cyanide poisoning. I have eaten them. They taste good."

Other members of the *Prunus* genus were used in a similar fashion, such as *P. subcordata*, also known as the Sierra plum, whose yellow to dark red fruit was eaten fresh or dried by various tribes, mostly in the northern part of the state. Some tribes removed the pulp of this fruit and dried the pulp into little cakes.

A view of the coffeeberry fruit and leaf Photo by Rick Adams

COFFEEBERRY
Frangula californica and *F. purshiana*

California coffeeberry is a member of the Buckthorn family (Rhamnaceae). There are fifty to fifty-two genera of the Buckthorn family worldwide, with about 950 species.

There are fifty species of the *Frangula* genus, with three species found in California. Aside from the two species listed above, there is *Frangula rubra*, or Sierra coffeeberry.

Description: *F. californica* and its six subspecies are most common in Southern California; *F. purshiana* and its three subspecies are found more commonly in the northern part of California. These are small shrubs to large trees, depending on location and species. *F. californica* is typically no more than 8 feet tall, whereas *F. purshiana* is significantly taller, very treelike. The leaves are alternately arranged, an inch or two in length, typically bright green, narrowly oblong, with tiny teeth on the margins. The fruits are green and turn red, then nearly black, as they mature. They are little globes up to ½ inch in diameter, with two and sometimes three seeds. The seeds closely resemble the seeds of commercial coffee.

Uses: Seeds used for a beverage; the bark for a laxative

Habitats: These are scattered widely in chaparral and woodland; in general, closer to the coast.

Range: Coastal ranges, with *F. purshiana* more common in the north, and *F. californica* more common in the south.

Tools: No special tools are needed for collecting the fruits.

Coffeeberry is a native California tree, found commonly (but not exclusively) in the chaparral regions. It's a beautiful tree, typically well rounded, with bright green leaves that make the plant resemble a gardenia. The oblong leaves have minute teeth on the margins. The fruits develop in the spring, starting green and turning red as they begin to mature. These fruits are nearly a half-inch in diameter, sometimes bigger in wet years. They are generally like little globes. When you squeeze a ripe fruit, you will notice the two, sometimes three, seeds, which resemble coffee beans. Though not related to coffee, the seeds are used the most from this plant. The flesh can also be used, but you need to be aware of its laxative effect. The main part of the plant used for medicinal purposes is the bark, which also has laxative effects.

Coffeeberry fruit ripening in the tree   Photo by Rick Adams

The berries are at the peak of ripeness around August, though this can vary somewhat depending on the season and locality. Collect the fruits when they are nearly black and the outer flesh is mushy. Collect as many as you can—I try to collect at least a gallon. Though there are many ways to process them, I usually just put them all in a bucket with water, and rub them between my hands to remove the outer flesh. Then I lay the seeds out to dry in the August sun. When the seeds are dry, I grind them in a coffee grinder. Then I roast them medium brown to dark brown. Finally, they are percolated just like regular coffee. This has a wonderful earthy and coffee aroma, very much like coffee's. The "coffee" itself is a bit more like strong tea or weak coffee.

It's a very good beverage and I enjoy it, especially when I don't want to be kept awake by caffeine. However . . . over the years I have served this beverage to many people and a small percentage have told me that they vomited an hour or so after our gathering. (Perhaps that's why some of them never came back?) It's true that the bark of coffeeberry has a long history as a laxative, and the seeds might have some of that same chemistry. Generally though, the drink doesn't affect most drinkers that way. But go slow the first time you try it.

Herbalists regard the bark of this tree as one of the safest natural laxatives. Native Americans have used it this way for generations, and it is one of the Native American medicines found in the US Pharmacopeia.

Since this tree is generally regarded as having laxative properties, I have always used the seeds with caution, and generally assumed the flesh of the fruits to be strongly laxative as well. The flavor of the flesh of the berries is unique and sweet, and you could call it an acquired taste. Some people like it, some don't. But I have never regarded it as a fruit that you'd

View of the ripening coffeeberry fruit

eat like any others, since it could be a laxative. I have eaten up to six fruits at a time with no ill effects and no laxative effect.

Lacking any hard data, I began to talk with wild food cook Pascal Baudar, and he told me that he has eaten as many as fifty of the fruits at a time, raw, and experienced no ill effects and no laxative effects. According to Paul Campbell, author of *Survival Skills of Native California*, the Atsugewi, Kawaiisu, Cahuilla, and others all ate the fruits of *F. californica*, *F. crocea* (the related redberry), and *F. rubra* (Sierra coffeeberry) when they ripened in late summer and fall. The Kiliwa crushed and ate the fruits and the seeds as a pinole.

Ripe and ripening currant fruits

CURRANT AND GOOSEBERRY
Ribes spp.

Currants and gooseberries belong to the Gooseberry family (Grossulariaceae). This family includes only the *Ribes* genus. There are 120 species of *Ribes* worldwide, and thirty-one species in California, not including varieties.

Description: These are vining or shrublike plants, often with many long and arching branches arising from a common root. Flower colors vary, depending on species, and can be yellow, orange, red, and more. The fruit is a berry, with small bristles in the case of the gooseberry. Generally, the petals form a tube, and when the fruit matures, the dried flower is often persistent on the end of the fruit.

Uses: The fruits are eaten raw, dried, or cooked and processed into juice, jam, and jelly.

Habitats: Species are found in the mountains, in chaparral, on flat plains, along rivers, and elsewhere.

Range: Common locally

Tools: No special tools are needed to harvest, though gloves are recommended with gooseberries.

Forager Notes: After a fire, or when the branches of the currants have been cut down, the plant sends up very straight stalks. These long straight stalks, a bit thicker than a pencil, can be cut and used as arrow shafts, just like in the old days. Currant gets harder as it dries, and actually makes really good arrow shafts—better than average.

Currants and gooseberries are both members of the *Ribes* genus, and do look very similar, though there are some important distinctions. They are both perennial bushes with somewhat vining stalks that arise from the roots. When cut back or burned back, the plant will send up many very straight stalks.

The stalks of the gooseberries are covered in spines. The fruits of gooseberry are also covered in little spines. Currants, on the other hand, have no spines on the stalk or fruit. But both plants have the very same growth patterns, and leaves that look like a three-lobed mitten.

I prefer the currants because they are easier to collect and have no spines. But both are useful, and both have their adherents.

The fruits are small, but you can get a fair amount if you find a good patch and carefully pick away. You never seem to be able to gather as much as you want. For one thing, the fruits don't usually all ripen at the same time. Then there are birds and other creatures of the outdoors who know about the sweet fruits too. Collect just the ripe ones, and then schedule a time to come back and pick more.

Dry these fruits and use as a trail snack. They can also be crushed and made into jam or jelly, and even juices.

CURRANT FRUIT PEMMICAN

Take equal parts of dried currants and/or gooseberries (if you use gooseberries, you must first remove the skins), dates, and figs. Chop and mix thoroughly. Roll it like a sausage. Add a little flour if necessary. Cut off thin slices to serve.

Currant jelly on crackers Photo by Rick Adams

The original pemmican used by Native Americans consisted of dried and ground meat, into which was mixed dried and ground fruit, usually currants. This would be put into an animal intestine (much like making sausage), and fat would be added. This preserves the meat, though the flavor can be challenging to some.

Gooseberries are spiny, so they need some special treatment. The spines are not stiff like cactus spines, but they can still be a little irritating when you're gathering. You might consider wearing gloves.

When I have collected fair amounts of gooseberries, I would first just mash them all up in a bowl, and then carefully work the pulp through a sieve, leaving the spiny skins behind. The pulp is actually pretty good, and you can use it as is on pancakes. Plus, I've had jams that other people have made from gooseberries, and found them excellent.

Nearly all the native peoples of California used currants and gooseberries, raw or dried. You will find that the sweetness and the palatability varies from species to species. Some you may not care for, but none are toxic.

A view of the elderberry's flower cluster, fruit cluster, and leaf

ELDERBERRY
Sambucus species

The elderberry is a member of the Muskroot family (Adoxaceae). This family has five genera and about 200 species worldwide. Only two of the genera are represented in California, one of which is *Sambucus*. There are twenty species of *Sambucus* worldwide, and according to the latest classification, you'll find four types of elderberries in California:

- *S. nigra*, subspecies *caerulea* (Mexican elder or blue elderberry), found at lower elevations, throughout the chaparral. The fruit is nearly black when ripe, with a white glaucous coating making it appear blue.
- *S. racemosa*, which has red or purplish-black fruits
- *S. racemosa* var. *melanocarpa* (black elderberry), found at higher locations and having purplish-black fruits
- *S. racemosa* var. *racemosa* (red elderberry), having red fruits, and preferring moist areas

Description: The different varieties of elderberry (elder) can be found in the dry chaparral regions of California, along streams, and in the higher mountain regions. They are generally small trees, with oppositely arranged, pinnately divided leaves with a terminal leaflet. Each leaflet has a fine serration along its edge. The plant is often inconspicuous in the chaparral, but is very obvious when it blossoms, with many yellowish-white flower clusters in the spring.

Uses: Flowers are used for tea and food; berries for "raisins," jam, jelly, and juice.

Habitats: Chaparral, mountains, desert, urban fringes, and generally in most environments

Range: Elder can be found throughout the state; it is widespread and common.

Tools: Snippers and bags

Sambucus nigra is the same elderberry that is routinely eaten in Europe, Asia, Africa, and South America. In Europe you can buy elderberry jam, candy, pastries, wine, liqueur (St-Germain) and cold medicine (Sambucol).

Elderberries are widely enjoyed throughout the country in a variety of recipes. Yes, you can just nibble on some of the little fruits as you collect them, but you should always go slow and cautious with elderberries at first. It is not advisable to eat any of the red fruits. Though some people claim that they can eat the red fruits without sickness, many do get sick by eating the red ones. Better to avoid them entirely, unless you really don't mind the prospect of vomiting by the side of the road.

In general, the darker fruits from higher elevations are less likely to cause any illness if eaten raw, but it's always better to go slow, just to see how your body reacts. The raw fruits are a bit on the sour side, with a low sugar content, which means that they will make a good dry wine, if you enjoy homemade wine.

To be safe, I suggest always drying or cooking elder fruits before eating. For drying, I collect as many clusters as possible, wash them, and then remove all the stems very carefully. Then I lay them out on a cookie sheet and let them dry in the oven at pilot-light temperature, or I lay them in the sun. The berries shrivel a bit when dried, and the flavor is good.

You could also powder the dried berries and use them as a sweetener for other foods.

Juice is easy to make from elder fruits. Collect, wash, and destem all the berries. Then mash them in a big pan with a potato masher. Pour through a sieve to remove the seeds. Then you can just bottle, chill, and drink.

However, after one of my wild food cooking classes in which we consumed elder juice, one man ended up in my front yard vomiting for about an hour. Two other people told me they vomited later in the day. Now, to be fair, there were other foods that, combined with the raw elder juice, could have caused the vomiting. The man in the front yard drank maybe two cups of the raw elder juice because he said it tasted so good. Though raw elder juice does not affect me that way, I have learned to always simmer the juice in a pan before serving to others.

The Pomo, Bear River Band, Atsugewi, Yokut, Miwok, Chumash, Gabrielino/Tongva, and Cahuilla were known to have used elder fruits, often fresh, but also dried for winter use. The Atsugewi mixed mashed

Forager Notes: The stalks of elder have a soft pith that can be easily reamed out with a metal wire. Depending on the length and thickness of the elder branch you cut, you can make it into a blowgun, a pipe stem (the type that is used on a calumet-style pipe), a straw (for stoking fires), or a flute. You could also cut an L-shaped stem to make a pipe. The thicker bark on the older (or dead) branches can be removed and shredded for a good quality tinder for fire-starting.

Elder flowers

elderberries with manzanita flour, added water, and made cakes, which they dried for future use.

The elder tree flowers in early spring, and produces its fruit in summer. Before the fruits develop and mature, elder trees develop their flat-topped clusters of yellow flowers. In many parts of the rural United States, the flowers are traditionally used as an herbal medicine for flus and colds of the spring. The fresh or dried flowers are simply infused.

Additionally, the entire flower clusters are eaten. They are first dipped in a tempura batter, and then deep-fried.

Ripening cultivated grapes

GRAPE (WILD)
Vitis spp.

Native wild grapes belong to the Grape family (Vitaceae). The Grape family has about fifteen genera and about 800 species worldwide. In California, this family is represented by only two genera, *Parthenocissus* (the Virginia creeper) and *Vitis* (grapes). Though there are sixty-five known species of *Vitis*, it is only represented in California by three species, one of which is the introduced cultivated grape (*V. vinifera*). The other two are the California wild grape (*V. californica*) and the desert wild grape (*V. girdiana*).

Description: Anyone who has ever grown grapes, or visited a vineyard, can automatically recognize our two wild grapes. Typically growing along streams or in moist canyons, these are sprawling, vining plants that often cover entire hillsides and whatever other vegetation is growing there.

You can usually see peeling bark on the woody stems, and you'll see tendrils opposite each leaf. The bottom of the young leaf is tomentose (covered with fine hairs), and is less so as the leaf matures. The fruit clusters tend to be more sparse

Immature wild grapes. Note the fruits are smaller than cultivated grapes.

than found on cultivated grapes, and sometimes (depending on the location and the season), there is a lot of leaf and vine and very little fruit.

Uses: Fruits are eaten raw or cooked; the leaves used in Middle Eastern cooking.

Habitats: Prefers riparian areas and moist, shady canyons

Range: Widespread in localized areas

Tools: Clippers, bags

When most people look at long grapevines sprawling over moist hillsides, they just stare for a few minutes as it starts to sink in that they're looking at a very familiar plant.

There are two foods that we get from the native grape: the leaves and the fruit. Let's start with the leaves.

If you've ever eaten Middle Eastern food, you've undoubtedly had "grape leaves" (often known as dolmas) with either rice or rice and some meat (typically lamb) wrapped in a grape leaf. When our friends Julie and Talal got married, Talal asked me to work with him to make some grape leaves for the reception. He and I went to the local mountains, found some wild grapevines, and picked some of the very youngest leaves we could find.

We boiled the leaves, and cooked rice separately. Then we put about a tablespoon of cooked rice into the center of each grape leaf, and rolled them into the shape of fat, short cigars. These we packed carefully, side by side, into a large pot for steaming. They were steamed for about fifteen minutes, and we served them at the reception. Talal and I thought they were great, and thought it was a very successful dish, but some of the guests thought the leaves were a bit on the tough side and a bit tart.

As far as the fruit is concerned, fresh grapes can be eaten chilled, pressed into juice, mixed with other juices, made into jams and jellies, dried into raisins, made into wines, and added to other drinks and jams and preserves—these are the many ways in which cultivated grapes are used.

Wild grapes can pretty much be used in the same manner, except wild grapes are much more sour and have a lower sugar content. This means that wild grapes are usually not eaten raw.

Wild grapes can be dried into a tasty little raisin. They are definitely tastier when cooked, and most wild food cooks add a sweetener to these sour fruits, such as honey.

Throughout California, indigenous peoples ate the native grape, and it was used in many ways. Some, such as the Karok, ate the sour fruits mostly raw. Others, like the Tubatulabal, sun dried them into raisins, which could be stored for winter use. Others made juices and stews from the wild grapes. The Cahuilla of the desert (around the Palm Springs area) ate them fresh, but also made mush and stews, as well as dried them for later use. The Indians tended grapevines in many canyons and knew how to treat them with ash to get grapes to form. They then gathered in these canyons (oases) in the fall to eat grapes.

> **Forager Notes:** In 1769, Father Junipero Serra, exploring somewhere in the San Gabriel Valley, possibly near present-day Pasadena, wrote in his journal: "We found vine (wild) of a large size and in some cases quite loaded with grapes. We have seen Indians in immense numbers . . . They continue to make a good subsistence from various seeds and by fishing."

The fruit of the ground cherry (*Physalis crassifolia*) Photo by Trent Draper

GROUND CHERRY
Physalis spp.

Ground cherry is a member of the Nightshade family (Solanaceae), which consists of at least seventy-five genera and about 3,000 species worldwide. *Physalis* is one of the thirteen genera of the Nightshade family found in California. *Physalis* contains about eighty-five species worldwide, with seven species (not including varieties) found in California, four of which are native. At least one is regarded as a noxious weed, and one nonnative is the widely cultivated tomatillo (*P. philadelphica*). Thus, in the pre-Spanish days, the only ground cherries eaten by the desert indigenous peoples would have been *P. acutifolia*, *P. crassifolia*, *P. hederifolia* (and its two varieties), and *P. lobata*. The last one, commonly called the lobed ground cherry, is not common in California. The first three have yellow flowers, and *P. lobata* has purple flowers.

Description: This is an obvious nightshade plant when you see it. Ground cherry is a low, sometimes sprawling plant that grows to about a foot tall, maybe taller in certain circumstances. The leaves are typical lanceolate to ovate, often toothed. The five-petaled flowers are usually yellow, but sometimes purple. The most obvious feature of the ground cherry fruit is its enclosure in a papery sheath, giving it one of its common names, husk tomato.

Uses: The fruits are eaten when they mature, and are fully ripe in the fall. Otherwise, they must be cooked.

Habitats: The native species can be found in desert washes, slopes, rocky flats, etc.

Range: Desert regions

Tools: Bag for collecting

Sometimes called husk tomato; one species (cultivated) is the popular tomatillo. The ripe fruits were eaten by the native peoples living in the desert near the Colorado River. The fruits must be eaten ripe, or sickness can result.

These are eaten like tomatoes, and can be used in salsa, salads, soups, and stews. The Indians would more commonly cook the fruits into stews, often with meat. When there was a sufficient crop, they would be dried for winter use. The dried fruits would be used as a condiment, or to make sauces for other dishes.

In *Stalking the Wild Asparagus*, Euell Gibbons points out that varieties of *Physalis* are found throughout the United States. He shares a story

POHA PIE

Poha is Hawaiian for ground cherry, or *Physalis,* fruits. First, make or buy your own 9-inch pie crust. Euell Gibbons, in *Stalking the Wild Asparagus,* described his poha pie filling, which I tweaked a bit to make it more healthful.

Mix ¼ cup of whole-wheat flour, 1 cup of honey (or use a raw natural sugar—even try date sugar), and ¼ teaspoon of cinnamon. Once well mixed, add the juice of one lemon and just enough water to make a smooth paste, about the consistency of thin pancake batter. Mix in 3 cups of washed and husked ground cherries.

Pour the batter into the pie pan, and give it a crust on the top. Bake in a medium oven for about 45 minutes, or until the crust is light brown.

Gibbons suggests serving the pie with cheese or ice cream.

about finding it also growing on the island of Maui in Hawaii. He ate the fruit raw to quench his thirst and hunger. He also describes the fruit made into salads, jams, and preserves. As you might discover by reading Gibbons, he loved wild foods, but wasn't that particular about using only healthful foods. So his jams and preserves (like the recipes found in most cookbooks) are loaded with white sugar. You'd have to experiment if you want to use a more healthful sugar substitute.

Huckleberry in fruit Photo by Zoya Akulova

HUCKLEBERRY
Vaccinium spp.

Huckleberry is a member of the Heath family (Ericaceae). This family contains about one hundred genera and 3,000 species worldwide. In California, there are twenty-six genera. The *Vaccinium* genus includes more than 400 species in the world, with eight in California. In general, *Vaccinium* are referred to as huckleberries, blueberries, cranberries, and even bilberries, depending on the species. All are native, except *V. macrocarpon*, which is the common cranberry.

Description: These shrubs have alternate evergreen or deciduous leaves, which are broadly lance-shaped. The stems are trailing to erect. The flower's petals generally number four to five, with a corolla that is cup- or urn-shaped. The fruit could be red or blue, large or small, and have flattened ends. Generally, the plants with the most desirable fruits are the smaller shrubs, about 3 feet tall, with larger, sweet, juicy blue berries measuring about ¼- to ½-inch in diameter.

Uses: The fruits are edible.

Habitats: Found in the woods, usually coniferous woods, in clearings, moist areas, and shaded areas

Range: The *Vacciniums* are forest inhabitants, mostly found in the northern half of the state and into the Northwest.
Tools: A basket

Two species of huckleberry are found in California. California huckleberry (*V. ovatum*) is an evergreen shrub with hairy leaves that are 2 to 5 centimeters long, elliptical to lanceolate, and leathery. The five sepals are fused at the base. The fruit is black, about 6 to 9 millimeters long. These grow in the clearings of conifer forests, mostly in Northern California. According to some early historians, the Karok waited until fall, preferably after a frost, to eat these purple to black fruits because they were sweeter then.

Red huckleberry (*V. parvifolium*) is deciduous (rarely evergreen). Its leaves are 10 to 25 millimeters long, elliptic to ovate, and thin. Red huckleberries are most likely to be found in moist and shaded woodlands of northern California. These bright red fruits were eaten fresh in midsummer, when they ripened, by the Karok, Pomo, and Bear River Band.

The fruits of all species can be eaten raw or cooked. The flavor of the ripe fruit can vary from tart to very sweet. Huckleberries can be used to makes pies and cobblers, jellies, and preserves. The fruits can also be dried for later use, and used to make a fruit pemmican.

The dried leaves can be infused to make a tasty and nutritious tea.

CHERRY-HUCKLEBERRY PIE
Begin with a homemade or purchased pie crust. Blend equal parts huckleberries and wild cherries (seeds removed), and cook. You should not need to add water or sweetener. Add about ¼ cup of raisins. When the thickness is right, add to the pie crust. Top with pecans, and bake at a medium temperature until it's done.

Juniper in fruit Photo by Helen Sweaney

JUNIPER
Juniperus californica

Juniper is a member of the Cypress family (Cupressaceae), which has thirty genera and more than 130 species worldwide. Only seven genera are found in California.

There are about sixty-seven species of *Juniperus* in the Northern Hemisphere. In California, we have just five species of juniper, all of which are considered native, including the Utah juniper (*J. osteosperma*).

Description: Junipers are shrubs or small trees with thin peeling bark. The leaves are scalelike. The seed cone is 5 to 18 millimeters long, more or less round, fleshy and berrylike, and a shade of blue that matures to brown. The aroma of the cones has been described as ginlike.

Sometimes junipers are confused with cypress, but the cypress have larger, harder cones with angular edges.

Uses: The berries are used for food and medicine.

Habitats: Dry slopes, pinyon woodlands, flats, sagebrush areas

Range: More common in southern California, and found south into Baja California, Arizona, and other adjacent states

Tools: A bag or basket for collecting

Wild food researcher Helen Sweaney did a lot of experimentation with the juniper berries to test edibility. Some of her experiments yielded barely palatable flours made from the seeds. However, she indicated that the berries are not only edible, but delicious, if your timing is right. In the Vasquez Rocks area, she found that the berries were edible in May. In the Palmdale area, she found that the berries were good near the end of June and into July.

Indians of Central California reportedly took the fresh juniper berries and boiled them before eating. They would also take berries that were fully ripe and dry, and remove the seeds. The pulp was then ground in a mortar and eaten raw. I've read this was "said to taste sweet," though I have yet to taste any that fit my definition of "sweet." The juniper berries were perhaps mixed with other berries to improve the flavor.

Mostly however, the juniper berries were ground into flour and then made into bread or mush. This was how the Cahuilla of Southern California used the berries. The Kawaiisu ate juniper berries once boiled. Some berries were dried in the sun for approximately a week, for later use. Berries with seeds removed were ground and then sifted to obtain finer flour. The flour was sometimes mixed with water to form small cakes, and then dried. Apparently, when these cakes were dried on a base of the leaves of a native member of the Pea family, Spanish clover (formerly *Lotus purshianus*, now *Acmispon americanus*) for up to a week, it was said the flavor of

MEDICINAL TEA

Linda Bishop, an ethnobotanist and faculty member at Sitting Bull College, makes a great medicinal tea from the juniper berries. She first heats juniper berries in 1 to 2 cups of filtered water for five to ten minutes, in a covered pot. Then she adds 1 teaspoon of fresh lemon juice, and 1 teaspoon of raw honey. According to Bishop, "when the mucous in your nose, sinuses, throat, and lungs feels thicker than pea soup and as immovable as cement, you need some type of expectorant to thin the mucous so that you can cough it up or blow it out." This tea is good for that purpose.

the cakes improved. According to some ethnographic reports, the majority of the juniper consumed was in the form of these dried cakes.

Among the Diegueño (also known as the Kumeyaay, who resided in southern San Diego County), the fruit was used but considered a "starvation food," meaning they didn't care much for it unless there was absolutely nothing else to eat. Try it yourself and you may understand why.

Chumash apparently enjoyed cakes made from the juniper berries, which was used for both food and medicine. The Gabrielino/Tongva also made sweet delicious loaves from the juniper berries. The exact recipe or process to produce such a "delicious" cake has apparently been lost.

I have found that if I feel the onset of a cold or flu, chewing on a few juniper berries can help bring my body back to "normalcy."

The immature fruit of madrone Photo by Dan Baird

MADRONE
Arbutus menziesii

Madrone is a member of the Heath family (Ericaceae), of which there are about one hundred genera worldwide and about 3,000 species. Twenty-six of these genera are in California, of which *Arctostaphylos* (manzanita) is the largest. There are about 20 species of *Arbutus,* and the madrone is the only native species of *Arbutus* found in California.

Description: Madrone is a shrub or tree with reddish bark that is typically shedding and curling. The leaves are alternate, leathery, and evergreen. Each leaf is oblong to ovate, 4 to 5 inches long, with small and shallow serrations. The white or pinkish flower petals are fused into a very characteristic down-hanging urn shape. The distinctive fruit is round, about ⅓ to ½ inch diameter, and orange red. The fruit is papillate, which means it is uniformly covered with small roundish bumps.

Uses: The fruits are used for food.

Habitats: Typically found in conifer and oak forests, usually in the lower elevations

Range: From approximately Santa Barbara northward; more common the farther north you go. More common near the coast.

Tools: A bag or basket

This is a common wild bush or tree along the California coast, generally in the northern part of the state. It is more abundant the farther north you go, and somewhat common into Oregon.

If you've ever seen the strawberry tree (*Arbutus unedo*), sometimes used as a horticultural plant, you will see the resemblance between it and the madrone. The leaves are somewhat similar: The strawberry tree leaves have more conspicuous teeth, whereas the leaves of the madrone are a bit larger—around 4 inches or so in length, and the leaf surface is entire, or minutely serrate. The upper surface of the madrone leaf is bright green, and its bottom side is whitish.

Madrone has drooping bell- or lantern-shaped flowers, which consist of five sepals, five petals, ten stamens, and one pistil. Of course, the most conspicuous part of the madrone are the round fruits, about ¼ inch in diameter. They are round, maroon-colored, and covered with bumps. When you cut the fruits in half, you'll see five chambers. The texture is much more substantial than a strawberry. The fruit is on the dry side, mealy, and substantial. However, the sugar content is low.

Though it can make a decent nibble, the madrone fruit is definitely improved by soaking in water, and perhaps by cooking it and adding a bit of honey to make a cider.

The manner in which certain Central and Northern California tribes used madrone fruits are perhaps still the best ways to enjoy these fruits. The Pomo and Bear River Band ate the berries fresh, as well as roasted, parched, and stored for later use. The Miwok used madrone like manzanita, and made the fruits into a cider. This is done simply by soaking the berries in warm water for a while, straining out the fruit, and then sweetening the water with honey or some other sweetener. The Karok dried the fruit and reconstituted it later, sometimes mixed with processed manzanita fruit. The Yurok roasted the berries over a fire and ate them, which would be a great way to process these during a camping trip.

Manzanita fruit

MANZANITA
Arctostaphylos spp.

Manzanita is a member of the Heath family (Ericaceae). This family contains about one hundred genera and 3,000 species worldwide. Twenty-six genera of this family can be found in California, and *Arctostaphylos* is the largest genus. There are at least sixty-two species of *Arctostaphylos* in California (not counting subspecies), which we refer to as some sort of "manzanita." All are native.

Description: Manzanita have characteristically dark red- or maroon-colored bark, often with a shredded look. They appear as small trees or bushes. At least one species is vining.

The leaves are alternate, evergreen, generally round or ovate-shaped, a bit leathery, and stiff. The flowers are like little white lanterns or urns that hang from the plant, and the flower parts are usually in fives. The flowers mature into the round, reddish fruits. Fruits vary slightly in color, from an orange yellow to a darker maroon color. Some have a very sticky surface, and some are very dry on the surface.

Uses: Berries used for beverages or as a food additive; leaves for medicine

Habitats: Different species are found in the mountains, chaparral, on rocky slopes, throughout parts of the desert, and in woodlands.

Range: Manzanita can be found throughout the state.

Tools: A bag for collecting

When I first learned about the distinctive manzanita bush of our local chaparral, everyone said that the berries could be eaten, but no one had actually tried them. Eventually I learned that cider could be made by soaking the green fruits in either hot or cold water, and drinking it with or without a sweetener. After I learned about this, I would drop a few mature manzanita fruits into my canteen when hiking to flavor the water.

The fruit is a bit sour if you collect it young, and it turns out that lots of folks make some pretty good jam and jelly from the green fruit. However, in the past, the ripe fruit was collected when it was dark red or maroon in color, almost the color of the bark. The ripe fruit may or may not be sticky (depending on species), and there is often just a thin shell covering a hard seed. All fruits can be used, but if you collect the sticky fruits, more work will be required to keep them clean.

Among the Cahuilla, the indigenous natives of the California desert, manzanita was regarded as a primary food source. Both the Chumash people and the Gabrielino/Tongva ground the manzanita fruits and made both drinks and meal from it.

Though manzanita's use is somewhat of a lost art today, it was once an important food additive. Manzanita was used as a thickener (to make aspic) or a sweetener to other foods. It can also be used to make a pleasant beverage.

I gently grind dry manzanita fruit in a molcajete, and then strain out the powder, leaving the seeds behind. I add this fine manzanita powder to

BARBARA'S MOUNTAINTOP MANZANITA TEA

Add approximately 1 tablespoon of whole manzanita fruits per cup of water to a tea pot. Cover with hot water, and let steep ten to fifteen minutes. Serve with a bit of honey. The tea can also be served cold.

Manzanita's stiff, leathery, dull-green leaves

bread or pastry products. I add it to my acorn pancakes, where it acts as both a sweetener and a smoothener. You can use manzanita wherever you would use aspic or a thickener, such as in gravy, jellies, or sauces.

All the coarse meal that is left can be used to make a drink. Put it all into a pan, cover with water and simmer for about ten minutes. The water's flavor will be sour, though there is that hint of sweetness. Add an equal amount of water and sweeten to taste—usually a tablespoon of honey will do. The flavor is subtle and very refreshing.

If you need vinegar, you could concentrate this initial boiling of seeds and coarse meal, to produce a pretty decent vinegar substitute. It would make a good wilderness salad dressing.

The edible "little tomatoes" of the nightshade

WESTERN NIGHTSHADE, BLACK NIGHTSHADE
Solanum spp.

The four related species of nightshade discussed in this chapter are members of the Nightshade family (Solanaceae). There are seventy-five genera in the Nightshade family, and 3,000 species worldwide. Eleven genera—one of which is *Solanum*—are found in California. There are approximately 1,500 species of *Solanum* in the world, with eighteen found in California. Many are toxic, and many are good foods.

Description: *S. americanum* (aka *S. nodiflorum*), *S. douglasii*, and *S. xanti* are native nightshades; *S. nigrum* is not. *S. americanum* and *S. nigrum* are very similar and sometimes difficult to distinguish from one another. The very young plant resembles lambsquarters, except that the nightshade doesn't have an erect stem. Rather, it's more widely branched. Also, though the individual leaves of both nightshade and lambsquarters are quite similar, the nightshade lacks the mealy coating of the lambsquarters', and lacks the often noticeable red in the axil of the leaf, which is common in lambsquarters. The five-petaled white to lavender flower is a very typical Nightshade family flower, resembling the flowers of garden tomatoes. The fruits begin as tiny BB-size green fruits, and by August ripen into purplish-black little "tomatoes." We've eaten all of the four listed *Solanums* with no problems.

Uses: Fruits are used when ripe, either raw or cooked. Green fruits can be used if cooked (fried or boiled). The young leaves are boiled and eaten by people from Mexico (where it is somewhat popular and called "yerba mora"), the Philippines, and Hong Kong.

Cautions: Is it possible to confuse these nightshades with toxic species? According to many, the species we've listed *are* toxic species, meaning don't eat the green, raw fruits, and don't eat the leaves raw. Sickness is likely in either case. There are individuals who experience sickness when they eat any member of the Nightshade family, including eggplants, tomatoes, peppers, potatoes, etc.

Habitats: Common and widespread in chaparral areas, disturbed urban soils, and wild areas on the fringe of urban areas

Range: Widespread throughout much of the state

Tools: No special tools are required.

The western black nightshade plant is somewhat common throughout the chaparral regions, and is not uncommon throughout developed urban areas. I've seen some in the desert, some at the beach, though rarely in the high elevations of the mountains. It is sometimes even cultivated.

The leaves are very similar to the lambsquarters' in shape, and the two plants could be confused in the very young stages. However, the

The dark purple fruit and leaves of nightshade

lambsquarters tends to grow with a single erect stem, whereas the nightshade is more highly branched. Plus, the lambsquarters' leaf will show some tinge of red in the axils and on the stem as it matures.

Nightshade flowers are five-petaled (like all members of this family), and white to purple in color. The fruit looks like a small, green tomato when it begins. It's about ½ inch in diameter at most, and round. If you cut it in two, you'll see that its inner structure is just like a tomato's. Surprise, it *is* a tomato. They're both in the same family.

Sometimes these fruits are called huckleberries, though this is not the plant normally referred to as huckleberry.

The ripe fruits can be used in any way that you'd ordinarily use tomatoes: in salads, in soup, mashed for sauce in Italian dishes, dried. They're not particularly good, in my opinion, as a juice, like you'd have tomato juice.

The Pomo ate the fully ripe berries of the native *Solanum americanum* (also known as *S. nodiflorum*), often called black nightshade, and they were highly regarded. The Miwok were known to eat the raw ripe berries of the native *Solanum xanti*, commonly called purple or white nightshade.

The leaves of the western black nightshade are cooked in various parts of the world. Generally, the young greens are boiled, the water changed, and the greens boiled again before eating, with or without seasoning. In Mexico, the greens are referred to as *yerba mora*.

A view of the overall Oregon grape plant, with leaf and fruit

OREGON GRAPE (BARBERRY)
Berberis aquifolium

The Oregon grape is a member of the Barberry family (Berberidaceae), which consists of sixteen genera with about 670 species worldwide. Only three of these genera are found in California. In the *Berberis* genus, there are about 600 species worldwide, with only ten species (not including varieties or subspecies) in California. All but two are natives.

Description: This is a low-growing, medium-size shrub, though some are low-growing and spreading. Leaves are alternately arranged and pinnately compound. The leaflets are hollylike, with spines along their margins. Flowers are yellow and formed in racemes. The sepals and the petals are similar, usually in five whorls. The approximately ¼-inch fruits are bluish to purple berries, and are tightly arranged in clusters that resemble tiny grapes.

Uses: Fruits can be eaten, or made into wine, jams, jellies.

Habitats: Coniferous forests, slopes, canyons, oak woodlands, chaparral

Range: Found throughout California, but less common south of Santa Barbara.

Tools: Collecting bag

A beautiful cluster of the multicolored fruit of Nevin's barberry (*Berberis nevinii*), a close relative to the Oregon grape

Though Oregon grape can be found throughout the state, it is most common in the wild from Santa Barbara to the north. It is also planted as an ornamental, so it can be found outside of its native terrain. The fruits of all members of the genus are edible, and all California species are generally referred to as Oregon grape or barberry.

My experience with the Oregon grape is mostly as a trail nibble, though on occasion I have mashed a handful to use as a pancake topping. These small oval berries are tart and refreshing, high in Vitamin C, and make a good jelly when sweetened.

According to Cecelia Garcia and John D. Adams, authors of *Healing with Medicinal Plants of the West*, the fruits of all the members of the *Berberis* genus, generally all commonly called "Oregon grape," were eaten raw or cooked by most Indians wherever the plant grew. *Berberis*

BREAKFAST AT THE ROOT STUMP CAFE

Collect and mash fresh Oregon grape fruit. Serve it fresh on hot biscuits. (*Note:* The fruit can be frozen for later use, or dried and reconstituted when needed.)

A view of Nevin's barberry leaf, which is similarly pinnately divided but narrower in outline than the Oregon grape

nervosa's blue to purplish fruits were gathered by the Yana people of the Sierra Nevada foothills and dried, then ground into a flour that was used for a mush. Many of the indigenous California people made drinks from these fruits.

According to Paul Campbell, author of *Earth Pigments and Paint of the California Indians*, the fruits are especially useful in making the traditional blue pigment and paint.

A cluster of just-harvested, ripe, native palm

PALM DATES (CALIFORNIA FAN PALM)
(Washingtonia filifera)

The California Fan Palm is the only native of the Palm family (Arecaceae) found in the state, which we will primarily address. Worldwide, there are about 200 genera of the Palm family, and about 3,000 species. Palms are very conspicuous trees throughout California, widely planted as a street and park tree. Typically, there is the large trunk, which could be fat or somewhat skinny, and can rise about 65 feet (in the case of our only native, the California fan palm), or as tall as a five-story building (in the case of the Canary Island date palm, which is not native but has widely naturalized in California). Typically, fronds arise from the crown of the trunk. The fronds are either palmately lobed or pinnately lobed. The palmate leaves are formed on a stem, and these are the fan palms. The leaves can also be pinnately lobed, which are the long "feather" fronds. The fruits are usually drupes, and are generally—but not always—called dates.

California has two genera of the Palm family.

Description: The main trunk of the California fan palm rises up to 60 to 65 feet tall, and the dried fronds are often seen hanging down the stalk. The leaves are like "fans," with the stretched-out-like-a-hand leaflets arising from a common stem. The fruits are small and black.

Uses: Fruits of most palms are edible, fresh or dried. Dried fruit (minus the seed) is used in many dishes.

Habitats: California fan palm prefers wet areas, such as desert oases. However, because the palms are widely cultivated, they can be found throughout urban and suburban areas.

Range: California fan palm is restricted in the wild to the low desert. Though not widespread, the California fan palm is very common in certain locales, such as Palm Springs. But cultivated palms are found everywhere.

Tools: Usually you can pick the fruit off the ground. If you can't wait, you'll need a ladder.

Everyone knows the date palms, which produce the sweet and delicious dates that you can buy anywhere these days. Many are grown in the low desert of Southern California, not far from Palm Springs.

Though date palms are common in commercial orchards in the desert, they are not generally widespread throughout the state. And palms, generally, are very common in California. Our only native date is the California fan palm (*Washingtonia filifera*), which is most concentrated around the Palm Springs and the lower desert area. It is also planted as an ornamental throughout California. Though not as common as the Mexican fan palm, the native fan palm can still be seen widely throughout Los Angeles and other counties, often as an ornamental.

This palm was the hardware store of the Cahuilla people, who lived in the Palm Springs area and the surrounding desert. The leaves were thatching for the roofs and coverings of their homes and were used for sandal making. The leaf stalks were used for making fire. And the fruits, though small, are edible.

You can just pop the little fruits in your mouth, chew them, and spit out the seed, which is most of the fruit. The pulp is a little fibrous and sweet, but not as sweet as commercial dates.

According to Lowell Bean and Katherine Saubel, authors of *Temalpakh: Cahuilla Indian Knowledge and Usage of Plants*, each palm tree could contain as many as a dozen of the fruit clusters, with each one weighing from five to twenty pounds. These were eaten fresh, or were dried and then stored in pots for later use. Flour was made from the entire fruit, both flesh and seed. This palm seed flour was mixed with other flours and cooked into a mush. A beverage was made by soaking the fruits in water. Jelly was also made from the fruits. Bean and Saubel also report that the palm heart was sometimes used as a famine food, which was boiled before eating. It most likely involved killing the palm tree to get to the tender pith inside.

One method that I like is to boil a bunch of the black fruits in water—about 1 cup of fruit in 2 cups of water. The water has a unique, subtle flavor. The juice could be concentrated for a sweeter product.

Eat a few of the boiled fruits, letting them roll around in your mouth while you chew off the thin flesh. The flesh is sweet, with a good texture, and very satisfying. Every time I try it, I can see why this plant was so valued by the desert natives.

The prickly pear cactus fruits of California. Gather with metal tongs.

PRICKLY PEAR
Opuntia spp.

Prickly pears are members of the Cactus family (Cactaceae). There are 125 genera in the Cactus family, and about 1,800 species worldwide, mostly in the American deserts. Eleven genera are found in California; one of those genera is *Opuntia*.

There are twelve species of *Opuntia* in California, not counting varieties. All but two are native. We are mostly concerned with prickly pears—oval-shaped, flat-padded cacti—since these are the easiest to harvest, prepare, and eat.

Description: Prickly pear cacti are readily recognized by their flat oval pads, with spines evenly spaced over their surface. The cacti flower by summer, and then the fruits mature by August and September. The fruits mature in a variety of colors, ranging from green (less common) to yellow, orange, red, and purple. Each of these fruits has a different flavor, and was traditionally used in different recipes.

Uses: Young pads for food, raw or cooked; fruits for deserts and juices; seeds for flour. Nearly all species of *Opuntia* have a long history of being used for food.

Habitats: Typically found in the desert regions, but also commonly found in chaparral, dry fields, along the coast, and commonly cultivated

Range: Fairly widespread throughout the state, very common in certain areas, like the desert, chaparral, and where it is cultivated in urban or farm areas

Tools: Metal tongs, sturdy bucket, possibly gloves

Cautions: Occasionally, people have experienced sickness after eating certain varieties of prickly pear. In some cases, this is due to a negative reaction to the mucilaginous quality. According to Dr. Leonid Enari, the entire Cactus family is very safe for consumption. However, he would quickly add that some are much too woody for food. A very few are extremely bitter—even after boiling—and you'd not even consider using them for food. If you choose to experiment, just remember that palatability is the key. Any that have a white sap when cut are not cacti, but lookalike members of the *Euphorbia* group.

Though generally regarded as a desert plant, the prickly pear cactus is actually rather widespread. Probably the only area where you won't find it is in the higher elevations, where it could not survive prolonged periods of cold or snow. The prickly pear is perhaps one of the most widespread of the cacti, and easy to recognize. There are different species of *Opuntia*, and though they can all be used as food, some are definitely tastier and more desirable than others.

The pads are oval-shaped and flat, though maybe as much as 1 inch thick. This cactus can grow like a hedge, or bushlike. The pads are covered with spines as they mature, and at the base of each spine is a cluster of tiny glochids, which tend to be more miserable than the spines when they get into your mouth and tongue and lips. The *Opuntias* flower in the spring, and then the oval fruits develop. The fruits are first green, and then, depending on the species, mature green, yellow, orange, red, or purple. The peak of fruit ripening is generally September. Each fruit has its own unique flavor. My preference is the large yellow fruit, and the very tasty orange fruits.

To collect the fruit, I bring sturdy plastic tubs, dishwashing gloves that extend as close to the elbows as possible, and long metal salad tongs. Sometimes I also carry a long knife.

When I begin to collect, I put on my gloves and pick each fruit by grabbing it with the tongs, then gently twisting it to remove it from the pad. Then I carefully place it into my plastic tub. I put the fruits in carefully so they are not all mushed up and impossible to clean when I get home.

At home, I turn each fruit a few times over a flame on the stove, and then put them into the sink, where I will rinse each fruit and gently brush with a mushroom brush. Then, I cut each fruit in half and scoop out the inside fruit, which readily separates (in most cases) from the skin.

Typically, I put the fruits into a blender and blend it all into a slurry. I pour the slurry through a sieve, which separates out all the seeds. I freeze the slurry in small yogurt containers, or even small plastic bags. The cactus

DOLORES' SECRET TUNA-TOFU PIE

My wife Dolores used to make a delicious pie with cactus by mixing the seeded fruit with tofu. The two were blended approximately 50/50 to make a pie filling, and she would add some yogurt, and sometimes honey, all of which she poured into a whole wheat pastry shell. These cactus pies were better than anything we ever purchased at a store or restaurant, and were always a hit at our wild food classes. Unfortunately, I have never been able to duplicate her recipe. Some of my pies have come close, but there was something she did that made it "just so." Unfortunately, Dolores passed away in 2008 and took her secret with her!

slurry can also be mixed 50/50 with water for a delicious drink. You could make jams, jellies, pies, and various dessert items with the cactus pulp.

Of course, the prickly pear pads (nopales) have been used in Mexican cooking for centuries. The youngest pads are best, and they must be scraped of their little, hairlike glochids, and sometimes peeled of the skin if the pad is older. They are then cooked in egg dishes, stews, and many other ways.

Eating prickly pear has long been regarded in folk medicine as a way to deal with diabetes. Modern medicine has confirmed that eating the prickly pear cactus pads (or making juice of them) can help those who suffer from diabetes. (For additional scientific data, see *Prickly Pear Cactus Medicine* by Ran Knishinsky. This book provides scientific evidence that prickly pear cactus fruits and pads are useful for treating diabetes, cholesterol, and the immune system.)

The Gabrielino/Tongva and the Chumash were known to eat these fruits fresh or made into juices. The seeds were also dried and ground into a flour.

Rose hips of the native rose

ROSE HIP (WILD ROSE)
Rosa spp.

Roses are a member of the Rose family (Rosaceae), which contains 110 genera and 3,000 species worldwide. Species from forty-five of the genera are found in California. There are about 100 species of *Rosa* worldwide, which hybridize freely.

There are twelve species in California, not including subspecies. Nine of these are natives, including the common *Rosa californica*.

Description: Wild roses are thorny shrubs bearing commonly recognized, five-petaled roses that form into orange fruits.

Uses: The fruits are eaten raw, cooked, made into jam, made into tea; the wood is useful for arrow shafts

Habitats: Typically riparian but found in many areas; cultivated roses are common in urban areas.

Range: Wild roses are somewhat widespread throughout the state; cultivated garden roses can be found everywhere.

Tools: Perhaps gloves

Caution: Before you go wild rose collecting in your neighbor's rose patch, you should attempt to find out if your neighbor uses any "miracle chemicals" to produce beautiful, bug-free roses. Some systemic fertilizers and pesticides could get you sick. If in doubt, do without.

Roses are sometimes referred to as America's favorite flower. Less well known is that we also have wild roses throughout the state, typically growing along streams and near riparian areas.

If you're familiar with roses, you know the look of their spiny stems and their pinnately divided leaves with little fine teeth on the leaflets. The flowers of domestic roses are well known, their many colors and many petals, but the wild rose has only five petals, and does not have the broad diversity of color that you find in cultivated roses.

The fruits of both wild and cultivated roses are usually about marble size and typically reddish orange. Some of the fruits—called hips—are larger, some smaller. The wild rose hips tend to be round, maybe ¾-inch long.

Some of the hips are sweeter than others, and they are typically fibrous. Pick the fruit, split it down the middle, and scrape out the seedy insides before you taste it. If you like it, you can eat more for your daily dose of vitamin C—rose hips are considered one of the richest sources of vitamin C.

You can eat the hips fresh or dried. You can also brew some of the fruits into a broth or tea. Don't boil it though, just let the hips simmer in warm water. Sweeten with honey if desired.

BARBARA KOLANDER'S ROSE HIP SYRUP

2 cups rose hips
Water
Sugar
Lemon juice

Cut off the sepal ends of the rose hips, cover with water, and boil until the hips are mushy. Strain off the juice, cover with more water and repeat. Measure the resulting liquid, and add 1 cup sugar and 2 tablespoons lemon juice to every 2 cups liquid. Boil gently until it reaches syrup consistency.

According to Kolander, you can use this basic recipe for any edible wild berries.

The Cahuilla and Chumash people were known to have collected the rose fruits and eaten them raw. The fruit was widely used among California's native tribes, apparently mostly eaten raw.

Though it's mostly the fruits of the rose that are used for food, the flowers too can be consumed. Rose petals can be added to salads, or the sides of dishes for color and some extra vitamin C. Rose petals can also be infused into a subtle tea.

Fruits of the Salal Photo by Zoya Akulova

SALAL
Gaultheria shallon

Salal is a member of the Heath family (Ericaceae), which is the family that includes manzanita.

This family contains about one hundred genera and 3,000 species world-wide. Twenty-six genera of this family can be found in California. The *Gaultheria* genus includes about 130 species world-wide, with three of these species found in California.

Description: Salal is a native shrub, with ovate leaves that are finely veined. The hanging lantern-type flowers make the relationship of the salal plant to the manzanita very clear. The flowers appear in a line along the stalk, and then as the berries develop, they are likewise in a line along the stalk. The berries are dark purple to more or less blue-black in color. When mature, the end of the fruit has what appears to be a five-point indented star.

The plant is a low-growing to medium-size evergreen shrub, with either spreading or erect stalks. It grows in moist areas along the margins of the forests, in some cases being the most dominant plant. The leaves are alternate, ovate to elliptical, about 3 to 4 inches in length. The leaves are finely toothed, leathery, and conspicuously veined.

Uses: Fruits are eaten.

Habitats: Salal is found in mixed evergreen forests, redwood forests, and amid the northern coastal scrub. You typically won't find it in wetlands.

Range: Salal is found generally along the coast, from the northern extremities of Los Angeles County northward.

Tools: Just a container for collecting

The Pomo, Karok, and other northern California indigenous peoples are known to have eaten salal berries fresh. These were widely used and were prepared in many different ways. The berries were dried and formed into cakes, which were then saved for later. The cakes would sometimes be dipped into oil and cooked. Or, the cakes would be reconstituted by boiling, and then eaten. The fruits might also be mixed with other dried berries and stored for winter use.

Jam, jellies, and pies were all made from salal. The Karok also used the fresh fruits as a dye for basket caps, and among other tribes, a switch of the branches was used for making soap from the soapberries.

SIMPLE SALAL CEREAL
Dry the fruits, and mix in with cereal or granola mixes.

Serviceberry fruit and leaf Photo by John Doyen

SERVICEBERRY
Amelanchier alnifolia

Serviceberry is a member of the family (Rosaceae). The Rose family contains 110 genera and 3,000 species worldwide. Species from 45 of the genera are found in California. The *Amelanchier* genus consists of about twenty-five species, with two species, and two varieties, found in California.

Description: Serviceberry is a large shrub or small tree with deciduous leaves, often forming in dense thickets. The twigs of this native are glabrous, and the leaf is elliptical to round, with obvious serrations, generally serrated above the middle of the leaf. The flowers are five-petaled, white, fragrant, in clusters of a few to many. The fruit is a pome of two to five papery segments, berrylike, generally spherical, and bluish black in color. The shape somewhat resembles a tiny pomegranate.

There are also two varieties of *A. alnifolia*. Variety *pumila*, with fruits 8 to 9 millimeters in diameter, grows on open, often moist, scrubby mountain slopes from about 4,000 to 7,000 foot elevation. Variety *semiintegrifolia* has a 10- to 15-millimeter fruit, growing on open conifer or mixed evergreen forest slopes.

This one occurs in lower elevations, as low as 50-foot elevation, to about the same upper elevation as variety *pumila.*

Amelanchier utahensis is found in the San Gabriel and San Bernardino mountain ranges.

Uses: Berries are edible.

Habitats: Found in red fir forests and lodgepole pine forests, up to about the 7,000 foot level and occasionally in wetlands. Also found in open areas.

Range: Serviceberries are found in the northern two-thirds of the state.

Tools: A basket for collecting

Fruits of several species of *Amelanchier* were used for food by various Native American tribes, and all members of this genus are edible. Fruits ripen in late spring and into the summer. The Pomo ate these fruits fresh. The Karok ate them fresh, or dried them for later use. The ripe berries were mashed with water into a paste by the Atsugewi, and then eaten fresh; they also dried serviceberries for later use. Several of the western tribes were known to dry these fruits and then shape them into loaves for future use.

Serviceberries would remain sweet when dried, and could be reconstituted later when added to water. In some cases, this would be served as a sweet soup. With sugar and flour added, these fruits have been made into a pudding. The fruit can be dried, ground, and used in a pemmican mix.

ALL-WEATHER FRUIT LEATHER
Mash the fruits to more or less the same consistency. Lay out on a lightly oiled cookie pan, and let dry in the sun or in the oven at pilot-light temperature, making a good fruit leather for the trail or for snacks.

Wild strawberry flowers and leaves (*F. vesca*) Photo by Jean Pawek

STRAWBERRY
Fragaria spp.

Strawberries are part of the Rose family (Rosaceae). The Rose family contains 110 genera and 3,000 species worldwide. Species from forty-five of the genera are found in California. *Fragaria* contains twenty species worldwide, with three found wild in California, all native:

- Beach strawberry (*F. chiloensis*), found along the beaches and coastal grasslands mostly in Northern California and north to Alaska. The receptacle is 10 to 20 millimeters, and the leaf petiole is generally 2 to 20 centimeters long.
- Wood strawberry (*F. vesca*), found in partial shade in forests, throughout the state and down to Baja. The receptacle is 5 to 10 millimeters, and the leaf petiole is generally 3 to 25 centimeters long.
- Mountain strawberry (*F. virginiana*), found in the higher elevations in meadows and forest clearings. The receptacle is more or less about 10 millimeters, and the leaf petiole is generally 1 to 25 centimeters long.

Description: If you've grown strawberries in your yard, you will recognize these three wild strawberries. The leaves are all basal, generally three-lobed, with each leaflet having fine teeth. It looks just the strawberry you grow in your garden, but smaller.

Technically, the strawberry is an aggregate accessory fruit, meaning that the fleshy part is derived not from the plant's ovaries, but from the receptacle that holds the ovaries. In other words, what we call "the fruit" (because duh!, it looks like a fruit) is the receptacle, and all the little seeds on the outside of the "fruit" are technically referred to as achenes, actually one of the ovaries of the flower with a seed inside it.

Uses: The fruits are eaten.

Habitats: Wild strawberry prefers higher elevation forests and clearings.

Range: Found widely throughout the state, though more common in the northern California

Tools: Baskets

Wild strawberries are pretty easy to identify. When the average person sees one, especially if it's summer and the plant is in fruit, they will typically say, "Hey, look, isn't that a wild strawberry?"

Strawberries are so widely known that just about everyone recognizes them when they see them, even though the wild varieties are significantly smaller than the huge ones that can be found in the markets. Cultivated strawberries can be about 2—even up to 3—inches long! That's huge. By contrast, a wild strawberry is between ¼ and ½ inch long. A half–inch wild strawberry is a big one!

Though they may be smaller, the wild ones are typically sweeter, firmer, and tastier. Yes, it may take longer to collect them, but you'll find that it's worth it.

Forager Notes: Strawberry leaf tea (made by infusion), though not strongly flavored, is popular in many circles. It is high in vitamin C, and is a mild diuretic with astringent properties.

You use these in every way that you'd use cultivated strawberries. Eat them as is, dry them, make jams and jellies, put them on top of ice cream and pancakes, etc.

Various indigenous peoples ate wild strawberry (*Fragaria californica*) fresh, including the Karok, Salinan, desert Cahuilla, Northern Diegueño, Pomo, Yuki, and others.

The sand strawberry (*Fragaria chiloensis*) was eaten by the Wiyot, the Kashaya Pomo, and others.

Wild strawberry fruit and leaves Photo by Jean Pawek

The flower and fruit of the sugar bush

THE THREE *RHUS*
SUGAR BUSH, LEMONADE BERRY, AND BASKET BUSH

These three native plants are members of the Sumac or Cashew family (Anacardia-ceae). The family is often categorized as toxic because species of many genera will produce a dermatitis. The family includes poison oak, for example, but also mango and cashew. There are 70-plus genera, and about 850 species worldwide. There are six genera of this family in California. The *Rhus* genus is represented in California by these three species, all native. (Poison oak was formerly classified as a member of the *Rhus* genus, but is now regarded as belonging to a different genus, *Toxicodendron*.)

Description: Sugar bush and lemonade berry are both evergreen bushes with similar leaves. Sometimes the two naturally hybridize, making it difficult to differ-entiate. The fruits are very similar. However, sugar bush leaves are broader, shinier, and tend to be folded (sometimes described as "folded like a taco shell").

The basket bush is deciduous and more of a vining plant, sending out long stalks, often branching, with three-lobed leaves that are sometimes confused for poison oak.

Uses: The red berries of all used for making drinks or eating. Leaves of all are used for medicinal tea.

Habitats: The plants are found in the chaparral regions and into the desert.

Range: Common in Southern California

Tools: Container for collecting

These are three related native plants of the same genus, which we will discuss together because of the similar manner in which the berries are used.

Sugar bush: *Rhus ovata* has leaves that are somewhat folded, and red flower buds. Berries were mixed with water to make a sweet drink. The Cahuilla ate the berries fresh or dried, or ground them into flour for making mush. The white exudation on the fruit was collected and used as a sweetener. Clusters of the small fruits were also eaten once cooked in water. Chumash pounded the fruit, dried it in the sun, and ate it. According to Cecelia Garcia and John D. Adams, the primary use of sugar bush by Indians was to make a tea from the leaves for treating colds and other lung infections, and dysmenorrhea.

Lemonade berry (*Rhus integrifolia*): The Cahuilla soaked the acidic berries in water and made a lemonade-like drink. The Northern Diegueño would put a mushed-up leaf into the mouth while on long journeys to decrease the sensation of thirst. Gabrielino/Tongva and Chumash dried and ground the fruits of both the lemonade berry and the sugar bush. They then either ate it alone, or made into a beverage.

Basket bush (*Rhus aromatica,* formerly *R. trilobata*): The Atsugewi collected the ripe fruits and dried them. They ground them into flour, added flour made from the fruit of manzanita berries, and made a flavorful drink. The Cahuilla used the fruits fresh, made them into a drink, or

---

Forager Notes: The little fruits of all three of these plants can be sucked for a sweet-sour trail nibble. They also can be tossed into your canteen for a trail lemonade.

The fruits of *R. aromatica* or basket bush. Note the leaf shape. Photo by Debra Cook

ground them into flour for a type of soup, according to Lowell Bean and Katherine Saubel, authors of *Temalpakh: Cahuilla Indian Knowledge and Usage of Plants.* The long stems of the plant are important in the manufacture of baskets. The leaves were also used to make a tea to treat colds, lung infections, and stomachaches.

REFRESHING DRINK

Collect approximately ¼ cup of the very ripe, sticky fruits of any of these bushes. Add to a quart of water, and simmer at a very low temperature. Strain, and sweeten to taste for a refreshing sour lemonade. Alternately, you can add ¼ cup of fruit to a quart canteen of cold water, shake vigorously, sweeten, and enjoy.

Clusters of ripe toyon berries

TOYON
Heteromeles arbutifolia

Toyon is a member of the Rose family (Rosaceae). The Rose family contains 110 genera and 3,000 species worldwide. Species from forty-five of the genera are found in California. The toyon is the only species of the *Heteromeles* genus *(Heteromeles* is Greek for "different apple").

Description: Toyon can grow to be a medium-size tree, and is probably most conspicuous in the winter when it's covered with clusters of orange-red fruits. The tree is found in the chaparral zones, and often planted on the fringes of the urban areas. The leaves are leathery and ovate, with toothed margins. The tree is evergreen and can be a large bush or a small tree. Each flower, which forms in the summer, is white and five-petaled, about ¼ inch wide. The clusters of orange-red fruit ripen from about November into January.

Uses: Berries are cooked, dried, or made into flour.

Habitats: Chaparral hillsides, canyons, and slopes; sometimes cultivated

Range: Found throughout the state, mostly in the western half

Tools: Just a bag for collecting the berries

CHUMASH WINTER

Boil two cups of fresh toyon berries in water for a minute or so, and then pour off the water. Add just enough water to cover the berries, and put on a low heat. Add 2 tablespoons of honey, and some whole-wheat flour. Just add a teaspoon or so of flour, and add more if needed. Continue to cook at low heat until you have a thick consistency. Eat as is, or use as a pie filling.

Since the fruits mature in winter, toyon were highly prized by the native communities who ate the berries dried or baked, and mixed into other foods. They were highly prized by the Chumash and also widely used by the Gabrielino/Tongva. After all, there are few other wild fruits that do their producing in winter.

When I am on the trail during toyon's ripening, I collect several cups of the fruit clusters. It takes about half an hour to remove all the stems. Next, I rinse the berries well, since even if they appear clean, they have accumulated lots of dirt. I put them in a pot, cover with water, and bring to a boil. I let them boil for perhaps 10 minutes, until they have plumped up just a bit. I strain out the water, add fresh water, and bring to a boil again. This process removes the astringency of the raw fruit, and brings out the sweetness. After this second boiling, I strain out the water and taste one of the fruits without any sweeteners or flavoring. The fresh flavor is a combination of the low sugar content and sourness, akin to a kumquat or a raw cranberry.

During one of my Thanksgiving wild-food cooking classes, everyone found the boiled toyons likable. "They're sorta like cranberries of the West Coast," remarked one woman. I had to agree.

Sometime I dry the berries. The flavor of dried toyon is mild, an initial flavor like black tea, and then, as you chew the hard little fruit, you get a very pleasant combination of both sweet and sour.

Richard Toyon, who is a fourteenth-generation Californian, according to the official records of the Mission San Juan Capistrano, descended from the Parra clan of the Acjachemem nation, formerly known as the Mission Band of the Juaneño Indians. His family originates in what is

The immature berries of toyon

now the city of San Juan Capistrano. "The toyon fruit played a significant role in the Acjachemem diet," says Toyon.

Though there are probably a dozen common ways of preparing the fruit—ground into meal, made into a drink, made into a dessert—Toyon says that in Acjachemem get-togethers today, the fruit is cooked in a wok, fried and lightly seasoned, and served 50/50 with rice. His relatives have also mashed up toyon berries and served them on top of potatoes, with butter. "I also take dried toyon berries on my Scout trips, and sometimes mix them into the regular trail mix to see if the Scouts even notice it," says Toyon.

HORTICULTURALLY INTRODUCED
PLANTS

PLANTS GONE WILD

HIPs versus "hips"

There are many introduced ornamental plants that have solidly established themselves in California. Many of these produce edible berries or nuts. These are not natives, but they are here.

But what should we call these plants? Helen and I talked about this for a while, looking for a term that would describe these nonnative denizens. We thought of "FUN" plants, for "Feral Urban Neighborhood" plants, but that seemed to convey a misleading message, that introducing non-natives is somehow fun or good or desirable. Then Helen came up with the term HIP: Horticulturally Introduced Plants. That seemed to fit on several levels.

When these introduced exotics were planted, it was often because the gurus of horticulture of the day were pronouncing them as the greatest new thing since sliced bread. Grow these bushes and trees, and you too will be hip! Really! And lots of people fell for that idea. This is the "in" plant to grow this season, and soon your yards and backyards will fill up with new "hip" plants, with great colors and much to talk about at dinner parties. Sometimes the hip and HIP plants were edible and useful, sometimes not, as in the case of oleander.

And just like the idol worshippers who adore the newest rock star of the season, when a new plant comes around, the old one is forgotten. Maybe forgotten, but most of the HIP "hip" plants are still here, hip or not, and often they expand into wild areas.

And since we're calling these plants HIPs, it's worth commenting on the rose hip, which is the common way of referring to the fruit of a rose. I am not sure how the term "hip" came to mean fruit, but one theory is that the ovary of the flower enlarges as the fruit, and the enlarged fruit might seem visually similar to a woman's hips. Hmmmm. If that were the case, why isn't *every* fruit called a hip?

Regardless, the rose is one of the unique plants in this book, since there is a native rose (and so we included it with the native plants), but there are also many HIP roses. HIP roses are probably in everyone's yard—the commercial hybrids with multiple petals of all hues of the rainbow. Our wild rose is not a HIP!

The plants in this section are not what we'd call "wild" plants, though many have gone feral. These are bushes and trees that have been widely planted for landscaping streets or yards, and which sometimes survive well when they are no longer tended. All are commonly used as ornamentals, though the fruits are typically allowed to fall to the ground and then discarded as if they were just trash. I have observed every one of these plants in wilderness areas where cabins once existed. After the cabins were destroyed by fires or floods, these plants survived for years and decades with no human intervention. They are survivors. And that means if we grow these plants, they can provide us with food with very little work and care. Furthermore, they are probably already growing in or near your neighborhood, just waiting for you to discover and to appreciate them.

Some cultivated plants, which can also survive on their own, are so common that we decided not to try to include them—citrus, for example. Rather, we're including many ornamentals that are common, but are either not commonly known or not commonly used for food.

HIP, but not necessarily hip . . .

Fruit and leaf of the Eugenia bush

EUGENIA (AUSTRALIAN BRUSH CHERRY)
*Syzygium paniculatum (*formerly *Eugenia myrtifolia)*

Eugenia is a member of the Myrtle family (Myrtaceae).

The genus Syzygium includes about 1,200 species, mostly found in Australia.

Description: The Eugenia is an evergreen shrub that is typically manicured as a border hedge in urban yards. Left alone, it grows tall into a tree.

Uses: Fruit can be eaten.

Habitats: Commonly used in landscaping as a hedge. Can be a tall tree.

Range: Widely planted throughout the state

Tools: Basket or bag

Eugenia is a widespread hedge and bush tree used in yards and ornamental gardens, often to define borders. My brother and I would walk home from school in the 1960s and pass by a long hedgerow of Eugenia plants. The color of the fruit was attractive—a bright magenta—and the flavor of the fruit was sweet, with a bit of tartness. The texture was like strange, like wet Styrofoam, but tasty. We would chew on the fruit, suck the juice out, and spit out the seed. Sometimes we'd eat the seeds.

Later, we learned that Eugenia was brought into California from Australia, as were the widespread eucalyptus and acacia trees.

Someone once served fresh Eugenia fruits at a gathering I attended. They were very large fruits, which had been chilled and lightly topped with honey. They were very good. Eugenia fruits would also make a good jam and juice.

Sometime in the mid-1990s, an insect called the eugenia psyllid worked its way through a large percentage of the Eugenia bushes in California, causing the leaves to appear puckered up with lots of little bumps, and this was accompanied by a black sooty mold that formed on the honeydew that was excreted by the psyllids. Many of the Eugenias died off, but the bushes are still fairly common in Southern California.

AUSTRALIAN BRUSH DESSERT

Pick at least two cups of the ripe brush cherries. Remove stems, wash, and chill in the refrigerator (or a river). When chilled, drip honey over the bowl of fruits, and serve. I prefer the berries whole, but an alternate way to serve is to mash and then sweeten the fruit.

Harvested fruits of the *Ficus rubiginosa*

FIG
Ficus spp.

Figs are members of the Mulberry family (Moraceae). This family includes thirty-seven genera, and 1,100 species worldwide. There are only three genera in California, including *Ficus*. The *Ficus* genus includes about 800 species worldwide. The common fig is *Ficus carica*, and there are also many introduced ornamental species.

Description: *Ficus* can be a shrub or tree, deciduous or evergreen, with leaves that are characteristically lobed, or simple entire leaves. The fruit is the common fig, though some of the wild and horticultural varieties can have small round fruits, about a half-inch in diameter or so.

Uses: Fruits are edible.

Habitats: In the wild, figs are found in creeks, riverbeds, flood plains, and around old homesteads.

Range: These have naturalized in the Central Valley, Sierra Nevada foothills, San Francisco area, and throughout Southern California. The ornamentals are widespread throughout the urban areas.

Tools: A box for collecting

Fig   99

A mature *Ficus rubiginosa*

The common fig is believed to be a native of western Asia. The trees are deciduous, and can grow as tall as 30 feet. The tree is known to reseed and naturalize readily.

In areas of Southern California where there were once homesteads in the mountains, figs and other drought-tolerant plants were planted and have survived. They have spread by means of the fruit (probably in bird feces), and often when a branch washed down a river and took root. Horticulturalists know that the easiest and quickest way to propagate figs is to take a cutting, root it, and create a vegetative clone.

Though I have seen figs listed in some quarters as a "native plant," my research indicates that all figs got to California from somewhere else, and

> ### FICUS TART
> Buy or make a small crust for a miniature tart, around 3 to 4 inches in diameter. Collect small ficus fruits, clean them, and remove the stems. Crush with a potato masher in a saucepan, with just a little water, and cook at a very low flame. Add about 2 tablespoons of honey per cup of ficus mash. Let cook for just a few minutes, then scoop into the tart crusts. Bake at a low oven temperature (no more than 250 degrees) until done. These little tarts shouldn't take much more than 30 minutes to cook, but just check them to be sure. We've also used solar ovens for tarts, which are done in about an hour.

none are native. Yes, figs might be "hip" in your garden, and they're also HIPs.

In addition to the cultivated fig tree, which is common and usually obvious to most observers, there are also the common ficus trees. Ficus. Yes, that's the same genus as figs. But most ornamental ficus trees have unlobed leaves, and grow into grand trees with towering limbs and spreading roots. Some cities are famous for their ficus trees. The trees are often prolific fruit producers, though the sugar content is very low. You can pick a fruit up and examine it, and you'll see it's just like a regular fig, but smaller. Cut it in half and you'll see that the internal structure is just like that of a fig. Why? Because it *is* a fig!

You can eat ficus fruit just like figs: fresh, dried, or cooked into some dessert item. Several of us once made little tarts with ficus fruits. We collected the fruits, and mashed and cooked them gently with a bit of honey (see recipe above). We filled small pie shells with the ficus mash, and cooked it at a low temperature. The tarts were really delicious, and this was no doubt in part due to the fact that we did all the work ourselves from start to finish.

When I refer to "figs," I am also referring to the fruits of these ornamental ficus trees. Figs can be processed into a butter, and made into some tasty jams and jellies. The fruit of the ordinary fig is about 50 percent sugar, and the ornamental ficus contains considerably less sugar. These fruits also have mild laxative properties.

Fig   101

Mature ginkgo nuts in bowl

GINKGO
Ginkgo biloba

Ginkgo is a member of the Ginkgo family (Ginkgoaceae). This family consists of gymnosperms whose only living example is the *G. biloba*, which is why it is called a "living fossil."

Description: This is a smooth-bark tree, often growing upright in a very vertical fashion when young, and then producing a much larger angular crown as it matures. Each leaf is fan-shaped, and has the appearance of a fern. The leaves turn yellow in the fall. The fruits, formed only on the female trees, are covered in a light brown, fleshy coating that is very odoriferous. The nut has a thin shell that is easily cracked.

Uses: The seeds are eaten; the leaves are used for tea.

Habitats: This is a cultivated tree, planted as a street tree, in parks, gardens, and yards.

Range: Found in various counties throughout the state

Tools: A bag or box for collecting

The ginkgo tree was believed to be extinct, and was rediscovered in a Chinese Buddhist monastery in the 1700s, where specimens were being cultivated. The tree is regarded as sacred to Chinese and Japanese Buddhists. Since it was rediscovered, it has been cultivated and spread all over the world as an ornamental and street tree. It is popular because of its unique appearance and its relative resistance to insects and disease.

In Japan and other parts of Asia, the processed nuts are added to rice and stir-fry dishes. The nuts are high in protein and low in fat. The medicinal properties of the nuts, which you get by eating them, are said to include the release of stress and hypertension (the result of dilating blood vessels and increasing oxygen into the blood stream). The nuts are also reportedly good for pain and soreness, as well as an aid to digestion.

Yes, I have harvested ripe ginkgo nuts many times, and yes, I have to hold my nose. The fleshy tissue around the seed really stinks! Some people have learned to not mind the strong odor, generally reminiscent of fresh feces. You can get used to just about anything, and in time, you can learn to not be bothered by the "aroma" of the flesh around the ginkgo nuts.

Once collected, let the nuts and their soft outer shell dry, which makes the nut significantly easier to clean. The cleaned nuts are then best dried, which can be done in the oven at pilot-light temperature. I have dried them with their shells and without. I don't know if one way is right or wrong, and believe it is just a matter of preference. However, ginkgo nuts in the shell seem to keep a lot longer than the shelled and dried ones.

Once roasted, you can eat the ginkgo nuts as is. I have never eaten these nuts raw because of the foul odor. There have been some reports that the nuts can make you ill if you eat them raw (no doubt!), and that they must be boiled or roasted for about 25 minutes. You'll know they are done when you can easily break the thin shell with a nutcracker. The taste is akin to a bean.

SAMURAI SNACK
Shell and bake ginkgo seeds. Serve with a dish of rice and a side dish of a few salted plums.

The unique shape of the ginkgo leaf

Ginkgo biloba leaf extract has been subject to many clinical tests, and it apparently increases circulation in the limbs and in the brain. Apparently, this is why ginkgo seems to be helpful for improving memory and assisting with retaining memories. Suggestions that ginkgo can reverse dementia don't seem to hold up in clinical tests. Nor do the claims that ginkgo can cure cancer seem to be valid, so far.

An extract from the leaf has also been found to improve the immune system, and to protect the heart by clearing plaque from the arteries. In fact, the extracts are used for many ailments, such as headaches, asthma, kidney disorders, and more.

I have found that when I am experiencing a "slow day," ginkgo pills, or homemade tea from the leaves, seem to offer a subtle yet noticeable pick-me-up without the eventual slowdown that follows drinking coffee.

A branch of jujube

JUJUBE
Ziziphus zizyphus; formerly *Ziziphus jujuba*

Jujube is a member of the Buckthorn family (Rhamnaceae). There are fifty to fifty-two genera in the buckthorn family worldwide, with about 950 species. There are one hundred species of *Ziziphus* worldwide, with three found in California: the introduced jujube, and two natives, *Z. obtusifolia* (graythorn), and *Z. parryi* (Parry's jujube), which is not common.

Description: Jujube is a shrub or tree. The leaves are alternate, shiny, and bright green, elliptic to obovate. The fruit is fleshy, red to maroon, with a datelike seed.

Uses: The fruits are edible.

Habitats: This is a garden escapee, sometimes found in mountain or desert areas where a homestead once stood.

Range: Found in the wild in most counties of Southern California, and in some counties of Northern California

Tools: A bag or box for collecting

I've found jujube in the wild, but normally you'll find it in someone's yard. And the only reason I found it in the wild is because the area once had a house and orchard, and had since reverted to the wild.

I like the look of the jujube tree, and I enjoy the flavor of the fruit. Sometimes called Chinese dates, they do somewhat resemble a date, but are not related to palms at all. The fruit's texture is a bit on the dry side, not that different from a date but with a texture somewhat reminiscent of Eugenia fruit.

Jujube fruit is eaten mostly as is, either very fresh or allowed to dry a bit, until the skin wrinkles. Fruits collected in the wild tend to be smaller and firmer than the cultivated ones you'll buy at farmers' markets. Cultivated fruits tend to be less mealy, and have a lighter texture. The fruits of both are often allowed to dry slightly before being used, and this does create a slightly different flavor. Jujubes can be used to make tasty drinks, fruit jellies, and jams.

The darker the fruit, the riper and sweeter they are.

Ripe loquat fruits in the tree

LOQUAT
Eriobotrya japonica

The loquat is a member of the Rose family (Rosaceae). The Rose family contains 110 genera and 3,000 species worldwide. Species from forty-five of the genera are found in California. The genus *Eriobotrya* has about 10 members world-wide, with only this species found in California.

Description: The loquat is usually a small tree used in landscaping when an evergreen is needed. The leaves are large and leathery, up to 8 inches long, and pointed at the end. The yellow fruits are one of the first fruits to mature each spring.

Uses: The fruits are eaten.

Habitats: Sometimes found in the wild on the fringes of the urban areas, typically where there was a homestead or where a hiker spit out the seed
Range: Commonly cultivated. It is also found in the wild in a few counties of California, mostly southern California, and some in the San Francisco Bay Area.
Tools: Bring along a box or basket for gathering the fruit.

The loquat, also sometimes known as the Japanese medlar, is one of those fruits that seems to be everywhere, but hardly anyone knows its name, and most of it just gets eaten by birds or falls to the ground and rots. This smallish tree—perhaps up to 15 feet tall—is somewhat common in California. The loquat's native home is China, Japan, and North India.

This evergreen's leaves are broad, and pointed at the end, averaging about 8 inches in length. Each leaf is dark green on the upper surface, and the underside is lighter green, with a characteristic wooly surface.

The tree produces white flowers in the late autumn, and its golden-yellow fruits are one of the earliest to mature in the spring. They are small, oblong fruits that are about 2 inches long, give or take. The flesh is sweet

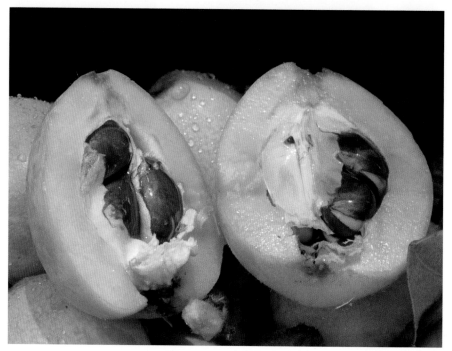

A view of the large brown seeds in the cut fruit

MARYSUE'S WORLD FAMOUS LOQUAT JAM

MarySue Eller, a professional Southern California cook, makes a fabulous loquat jam that she sells at farmers markets. I got her to tell me her recipe:

She begins with 4 cups of fresh loquats which she washes and deseeds. Then she puts them into a pot and adds just a little water, adds 1 to 2 cups of sugar (depending on what sweetness is desired), and the juice of one lemon. She then cooks it for one to two hours until it gets thick, and until it gets to 220 degrees f. Then she puts them into sterilized jars. MarySue advises home canners to research the details of proper home canning in a book or on a website that specializes in such things.

and free of fiber, and each fruit contains a few large, brown seeds. The flavor is sweet, but with a slight sour tang.

The fruit is great simply chilled and eaten fresh. You can remove the seeds, and serve a bunch of the fruit with some ice cream. Once the large seeds are removed, the flesh is sweet and tender and can be readily made into jams or pie fillings. The loquat is high in vitamin A, dietary fiber, manganese, and potassium.

Loquat syrup, made from the leaf, is used in various Chinese sore throat syrups, as well as for cough drops. The leaves are usually combined with other ingredients (honey for example), and the demulcent effect soothes the respiratory and digestive systems.

The seeds can be planted, and they readily sprout. It's pretty easy to grow new loquat trees, and they will produce fruit in a few years.

Mulberry leaves and young fruit

MULBERRY
Morus spp.

Mulberry is a member of the Mulberry family (Moraceae), which includes thirty-seven genera and 1,100 species worldwide. There are three genera in California. The genus *Morus* includes about twenty species. In California, *Morus alba*, the white mulberry, is most commonly found in the wild, and *Morus nigra*, the black mulberry, is more common in urban areas.

Description: The mulberry tree has alternate leaves, unlobed or three to five–lobed. The tree produces a catkin and then a fruit, which resembles an elongated blackberry. The fruit is technically referred to as a fruit of many achenes ("seeds") within the fleshy calyxes. Just think elongated blackberry and you'll get the picture. The white mulberry fruits are white to pink, and the black mulberries are purple.

Uses: Fruits are edible.

Habitats: In the wild, you'll find the white mulberry in disturbed soils, on the edges of streams, in moist areas, and in cultivated areas.

> **Forager notes:** Archers consider the long, straight branches of the mulberry tree ideal wood for carving a bow.

Range: These are most common in the great Central Valley and the Sierra Nevada foothills.

Tools: The fruits are fragile, so use a box or basket when you collect, *not* a plastic bag.

Pick mulberries and use them right away. They are best very fresh.

If you go to a nursery to buy a fruiting mulberry tree, you might not find one. Some years ago, nurseries started switching to nonfruiting varieties because, according to gardeners and homeowners, the fruits stained the sidewalks. Yes, that happens!

Where I once lived, there was large, old mulberry just outside the backdoor, and yes, it regularly stained the cement walkway. These were the white mulberries, and the stains weren't permanent. I tried to pick and eat as many as I could, and the neighborhood squirrels usually beat me to the fruit on the path.

The fruits of any variety can be collected when fresh and eaten as is. They can be dried too, but the fruit always seems fragile and is best eaten right away. Of course, jams, jellies, and preserves can be made with mulberries, so you have some later in the year.

SUMMER DREAMS
Serve fresh mulberries in a small dish of vanilla yogurt.

A ripe natal plum

NATAL PLUM
Carissa macrocarpa

Natal plum is a member of the Dogbane family (Apocynaceae). This family has about 1,500 species divided into about 424 genera. Many species are toxic, and many have white milky sap. *Carissa* is a genus that includes eight species, one of which is *C. macrocarpa*.

Description: Natal plum has shiny stiff green leaves and snowy white, five-petaled flowers that emit a pleasant perfume. The plant is spiny, and the fruit is an oblong berry with many small seeds. When you cut the fruit, you will see a white sap.

Uses: The fruits are eaten.

Habitats: The natal plum is commonly planted as an ornamental shrub.

Range: Commonly found in Los Angeles and San Diego Counties, and scattered elsewhere.

Tools: Container for collecting the fruit

Natal plum is a South African native, where it goes by the name of num-num. In other parts of Africa, the plant is known as noem-noem (slight variation), and amatungulu.

The five-petaled flower of the natal plum

Natal plum is widely planted as an ornamental in private yards, around schools, and as hedges. It's an evergreen that requires very little care and upkeep, which is primarily what professional gardeners are concerned with. The plant has rather stiff leaves and thorns, and hardly seems like it could produce a food. The fruits tend to be oblong, about 1 inch to 1½-inch long. The green fruit is regarded as toxic, so don't eat it. When you cut a fresh fruit in half, it exudes a white sap, which is a turnoff to most people because they have heard the old husband's tale that anything with white sap should be avoided. Of course, members of the Spurge family (most of which contain white sap) are not used for food, but there are many food plants that exude a milky sap when cut.

The fruit is sweet and edible, and most people like it. When ripe, the fruits are a bit tangy, maybe tart. These fruits have been described as rich with vitamin C, calcium, magnesium and phosphorus. They can be eaten as is, or turned into pies, jellies, and jams. The fruits are improved when chilled, and could be simmered or cooked in a variety of recipes that call for fruit, especially jellies.

A bowl of ripe olives, ready for processing Photo by Pascal Baudar

OLIVE
Olea europaea

The common olive is a member of the Olive family (Oleaceae). This family contains about twenty-five genera and 900 species worldwide. The genus *Olea* contains twenty species, and only this one occurs in the wild in California.

Description: The olive tree is evergreen, forming a medium-height tree that requires little care or upkeep. It often can be found along streets and in parks.

Uses: The fruits are processed and eaten, or pressed for oil.

Habitats: Found on farms and the fringes of farms, and in urban areas as a street tree and landscaping tree

Range: Widely cultivated throughout the state, and widely planted as an ornamental

Tools: Plastic buckets are the ideal container for collecting olives.

Olives have been valued since ancient times for their fruit and oil. Olives were brought to North America from Europe during the Mission era, and they have done quite well here. These are evergreen trees that are drought tolerant and require very little care. Because of this, they are widely planted in parks, along streets, on school campuses, and in housing complexes where a "California look" is desired.

When olives are used as landscaping trees, their fruits are largely ignored, fall to the ground, and raked away. If you pick up such an olive and taste it raw, it's astringent and not flavorful.

How are they prepared for consumption?

One common method for processing olives is with lye—the same lye that you could use to help open clogged drains, which you need to wear gloves for because the lye is so caustic. I have processed olives with lye many times, but never liked using such a dangerous product to produce an edible food. I wondered if lye would have been used hundreds of years ago in Europe and the Middle East when they processed olives?

It turned out that peoples of the past processed their olives using only salt. Today, I only process olives using salt, and here is an example of what I do.

I select olives that are not bruised. Once I collect the olives, I wash them. Sometimes—but not always—I pit the olives using an olive pitter, a device that is not common. I generally try to process as many olives as possible, and generally end up processing about a gallon of olives at a time.

I put them into a plastic or glass container, depending on what is handy. I dissolve one full (round) box of salt (26 ounces) in water, and pour it over the olives. This is a very salty brine, and I just let the bucket sit for about two weeks. I place a cheesecloth cover over the bucket to keep out bugs and dirt.

After two weeks, I pour off the water, rinse the olives, and then add water in which only a half box of salt has been dissolved,. This time I let it set for just a week. At this point, you can begin to taste the fruits to see if they are OK to eat. Generally, I do at least one more weak brine solution before the olives are ready to eat. I pack them into glass jars with a little salt, some garlic and other seasonings, and refrigerate them. They seem to last for years this way—I've had some that were more than ten years old and were still good.

Of course, if you don't want to refrigerate, you need to do proper canning, and you can read books and take classes that will teach you how to do canning safely.

OLIVE OIL

You make olive oil by pressing olives to express the oil, and then letting dirt and water settle out. Once the oil has settled, you can readily filter out any dirt and any water. That's really all there is to it!

The first time I processed a batch of olive oil, I used an Acme food processor and juicer. My friend David Arzouman and I first removed the pits from each olive. Obviously, in commercial operations, this is not done, but we felt we should do it for our small experiment.

We carefully packed the olive pulp into a large cloth container, and then put it into the processor and turned it on, so that it began to press on the pulp. We did this slowly, and eventually a clear liquid flowed from the machine. We collected about two cups of pure olive oil, and discarded the pulp.

We let our oil settle in a glass jar. Within an hour or so, a little debris was floating on the top, which we easily removed. We carefully divided the clear pure oil into two containers so we could both take some home to use. It had a remarkably clean flavor. It worked well in salad dressing and for sautéing eggs. Both David and I found it to be the best olive oil we've ever had.

Based on the grading scale used by the olive oil industry, the pure clean oil that David and I produced would be considered extra virgin olive oil—the very best!

One of the best sources of information on the home processing of olives is a pamphlet called "Home Pickling of Olives," published by University of California, Cooperative Extension, Berkeley, CA 94720.

The fruit and leaves of the common pyracantha shrub

PYRACANTHA
Pyracantha angustifolia

Pyracantha, also known as firethorn, is a member of the Rose family. The Rose family contains 110 genera and 3,000 species worldwide. Species from forty-five of the genera are found in California. The *Pyracantha* genus contains ten species worldwide and at least three can be found in California, all introduced. *Pyracantha angustifolia* is perhaps the hardiest species, and can sometimes be found in the wild, having gone feral.

Description: Pyracantha is commonly planted as a hedge or border bush, though it can grow much taller than a hedge. The fruits—orange or red—are most conspicuous. They are about ¼ inch in diameter. The leaves are obovate, and the plant is spiny. It can be found in most nurseries.

Uses: Fruits are eaten various ways.

Habitats: Most common along the coast; cultivated as a hedge and ornamental, and often escaped to the wild

Range: Found throughout the state

Tools: A bag or box, and gloves

A close-up of some pyracantha fruit

The pyracantha is commonly used as an urban hedge. I've seen it grow quite tall—almost like a tree—but generally it is tamed down to a hedge about 4 feet tall. You don't really notice it unless it's in flower, or when its striking red-orange fruits are ripe.

Or until you trip or get pushed into the hedge, with its many thorns!

The fruits resemble little apples, and I recall my mother telling me never to eat the fruits of this bush that grew outside our home. She said they were poisonous, and the evidence of this was that supposedly birds have been noted to eat the fruits and then fly around erratically. Really?

Had my mother actually seen such a bird? Well, no, she admitted, but she'd heard about it, and was sure that others had seen that too.

But so what? That doesn't have any relevance to humans. When properly prepared, humans can eat these fruits without the aftereffect of flying erratically.

Raw pyracantha berries are not particularly flavorful. They are dry and astringent. Squeeze one and it will reveal its somewhat dry insides. Occasionally you might find a raw one that is better than average. But if you're going to eat these fruits, it's best to cook them and prepare them as sauces, jams, and jellies.

To make jams or jellies, pick and wash the fruits and then cook them, changing the water at least once. Add sugar and cook some more, until the desired thickness is obtained.

I've had some of these fruits simply dried and used as a trail nibble. They are OK, nothing really exceptional, but you might have a different opinion.

PYRACANTHA JELLY

In the February 1976 issue of *Desert Magazine*, Helen Peterson describes her experiments with making pyracantha jelly and came up with a recipe that all her friends liked.

Peterson first collects 3 quarts of the berries and washes them. She puts them into a pot with 3 cups of water, and boils for twenty minutes.

Then she adds the juice of one grapefruit and the juice of one lemon, and strains it all through a jelly bag to get rid of all the pulp. This results in about 3½ cups of juice. Then, she adds one box of powdered pectin, and brings the jelly to a boil. She adds 4½ cups of sugar and a pinch of salt, and brings to a full boil for 3 minutes. She then pours the rosy pink jelly into sterile jars, which Peterson seals with paraffin.

Nowadays, everyone is concerned about the use of white sugar, which has no nutritive value and is the cause of so many diseases. Since this recipe is so heavy on the white sugar, you might experiment with other sweeteners, such as honey, maple syrup, or even date sugar.

INDEX

RECIPE INDEX

ABOUT THE AUTHOR

Christopher Nyerges, cofounder of the School of Self-reliance, has led wild food walks for thousands of students since 1974. He has authored ten books on wild foods, survival, and self-reliance, and thousands of newspaper and magazine articles. He continues to teach and lecture about wild foods and self-reliance issues. He and his wife, Helen, live in Los Angeles County, California.